BRAVER THAN YOU THINK

How to help your child with a disability live their best life

EMILY HAYLES

'This respectful and supportive book is a must-read manual for those parenting a child with disabilities to live their biggest life. The steps towards becoming BRAVE as a parent are outlined in a practical and empowering way. Emily and her beautiful wisdom and words are there on the journey with you every step of the way.'

Cathy Love, Allied Health Business Coach, Occupational Therapist, Speaker, Author

'Emily's approach to encouraging parents to seek the early intervention their children might need, even if it's just trusting your gut instinct, is summed up beautifully in this book. If your child has a developmental delay with or without a name, or even a genetic diagnosis that seems scary, and is not one of those mentioned, Emily's BRAVE model is still an essential element for any parent who has a child who requires that little extra help to grow and develop to their full potential. Her ideas can be applied at any stage on your family's journey, and the best part is that her advice and experience is that gentle voice of encouragement that you might need to hear…that "yes there is help out there, and a diagnosis is just a word".'

Julianne Schmid, Mum of two boys with Usher's Syndrome

'Emily has recognised a gap in the journey of families with children who have a disability. Her many years of experience working as a Physiotherapist in Paediatrics has enabled her to travel the winding road of a diagnosis and the difficulties families face along the way once their child has been diagnosed. Emily has written an informative and practical book based on current research and experience about child development and the concerns that parents encounter. Emily discusses the importance of early intervention and that "diagnosis is not prognosis", and offers many useful case studies as examples. This is a necessary read for any parent at the beginning of their "diagnosis" journey as to the best ways they can navigate a range of people and places.'

Barb Carroll, Principal Education Officer – Student Services, Department of Education – Queensland

'As a mother of a two-year-old little girl with Koolen De Vries Syndrome (17q21.31 microdeletion syndrome) it is my wish that not only every parent who has a child with a disability can read this book but that every parent can read it. *Braver Than You Think* is an invaluable resource for any parent who recognises developmental delays in their child. It addresses not only the concerns we as parents have for our children's development and future but also guides you on how to support your child, the importance of early intervention, how to find the balance in your family life once again and also where and when to seek help. I love the BRAVE concept and how the book is structured. It's not easy – as Emily mentions – to support a child with a disability or delay but I am excited to have a tool such as this on the days I feel a little lost.'

Amy Forrester, Mum to Juliet, aged 2 years, Koolen De Vries Syndrome

'*"You are a powerful voice for your child."* Emily captures an important concept that all parents need to know and embrace, especially if you have a child with special needs. My relationship with Emily began when my son, Conrad, was four weeks old. Conrad, now 12, has Down syndrome (Trisomy 21), and Emily has demonstrated her belief of all children having value and being given the opportunity to realise that value at each appointment. This is the book that would have been very useful when Conrad was born and will be my newest resource to help achieve the best life possible for Conrad. *Braver Than You Think* will set any parent concerned about their child's development on the right path for seeking assistance for their child and ensuring the best fit for their family.'

Anne Borg, Mum

'Wow! I have a huge network of friends with kids with different abilities, and as I read this book so many things I have heard along the way from their experiences were explained thoroughly. What a fantastic resource for those new to their journey to understand the importance of early detection and intervention. From personal experience, I found guilt went hand in hand with the grief and loss

… As I grieved the loss of the child and life I was expecting, I felt mummy guilt on so many levels: was I doing enough for him, how could I be grieving when I was lucky to have my child, and now how can I spread my time between being a mum, housewife, parent of a child with so many therapy demands and meet my other child's needs? I also got caught in a sea of denial that my child wouldn't be as badly affected by his disability as others were. I got caught in the "I don't have it that bad compared to others" cycle, not realising minimising my own feelings actually wasn't the best for my mental health. I read so many books upon his diagnosis; I wish this was something someone told me in the early days is totally normal, natural and understandable. I wish someone warned me of the changes in family dynamics, the jealousy and anxiety around seeing my friends' typically developing kids. I wish I anticipated my friendships would change, and that my whole life perspective might change. I resisted being that "special mum"; I wish I reached out to new friends earlier. I feel like my son's birth defined a new chapter of my life, and unveiled a precious appreciation of life. As I created my friendship and community circle I found all of the above feelings were extremely common.

'Well done to Emily for creating this resource, and well done to her readers for empowering themselves with knowledge.'

Bec Nicol, Founder All Abilities Mackay Inc, Summer House Mackay, and Down syndrome Mackay

'Growing up with a younger sister who had Cerebral Palsy (GMFCS level 5), I remember my parents and myself were faced with an overwhelming amount of therapy and doctors' appointments. Constantly feeling like none of the therapists understood how hard every day was. That even things that seemed simple were a very real challenge. And that some days, absolutely everything felt like a struggle. My sister is the reason I am a Physiotherapist today. Her life, and growing up with her, birthed a desire in my heart to work with children with disabilities. My passion is to help families journey through life and understand that their child can live an amazing life – their best life.

Braver Than You Think does exactly that! It journeys with the family through the BRAVE acronym, focusing on the child as a whole and how by doing that it will change the way you view therapy. The underlying philosophy of this book will leave you feeling confident and empowered to ask the right questions and know that your child is more than their diagnosis, allowing them to live their best. Your child's best will not, and should not, look like another child's best life. Emily helps the reader to understand each child's potential by exploring real-life case studies of children she has worked with and how each family was creating "their best life". If you have a child with a disability, know someone with a disability, or are a therapist working with kids with disabilities, I *strongly* encourage you to read this book. You will leave with a new perspective on what it means to live your best life.'

Delia Weston, DPhty BSc, Senior Physiotherapist at Allsorts Developmental Services

'In *Braver Than You Think*, Emily has put together a comprehensive guide for parents who come across the journey of looking after a child with a disability. Emily is a very experienced physiotherapist in regional Queensland and business owner and team leader of one of the largest allied health groups in the region. Through her book she is sharing her expertise as well as her experience of living this journey daily with parents. Her aim is to empower and enable parents to understand the science as well as how to manoeuvre through the support systems with confidence. I like the way she has combined case examples and literature reviews, in a contemporary and heartfelt way, making her advice resonate with all parents and carers. A must read for anyone on the child development journey, I would highly recommend this book to all my patients, friends and colleagues.'

Dr Michalis Yiallourides, Paediatrician

*All children – regardless of their ability
or disability – have value and should be given
the opportunity to realise that value.*

Emily Hayles

About the author

Emily Hayles is an experienced physiotherapist who has worked with children with disabilities and their families since 2006. She is the founder of Move and Play Paediatric Therapy, a leading children's therapy service based in Mackay, Queensland, Australia, and the Mum of two small children.

Throughout her career, Emily has had the privilege of listening to, learning from, and helping hundreds of children with a disability and their families, in a variety of clinical and research settings. In 2014 Emily completed her Masters of Physiotherapy through Research, where she investigated parents' experiences of health care for their children with cerebral palsy and published three articles in peer-reviewed academic journals and presented the results of her research at three national and international conferences. As an experienced clinician and leader, Emily is a sought-after educator for both clinicians and families alike, providing regular mentoring for therapists, contributing informative guest articles for national clinical and parenting websites, and being invited to present education sessions for parents within her local community.

At Move and Play, Emily leads a small team of likeminded therapists, who are equally as passionate about helping children with developmental delays and disabilities. Working together with children, their families, and other services within the community, Emily and her team help children to move and play to the best of their ability and empower parents to know they are doing the best they can for their child through therapy, education, advocacy and connection.

About the author

Emily believes that parents know their children better than anyone else and are the key to helping their children achieving amazing outcomes and living their best life. In this book, Emily brings together her professional knowledge, the stories and experiences of children and families, and her personal experience as a Mum, to share what she has learnt about how parents can help their child with a disability be the best they can be.

For more information please visit: www.moveplaypaedtherapy.com.au, or follow Move and Play Paediatric Therapy on social media (Facebook: www.facebook.com/moveplaypaedtherapy/; Instagram: www.instagram.com/moveplaypaedtherapy/?hl=en).

Acknowledgements

This book would not have come into existence without support, understanding, and inspiration generously shared from many people:

To Mike Reid and Mike Clarke from Dent Global – thank you for helping me to realise that "I am standing on a mountain of value" and planting the seed in my mind about writing a book.

To everyone who provided me with feedback on the BRAVE model when I was first developing it, but a special mention to Anna, Rachael, Kay N, Michael, Mat, Mike R, and Mike C. It took me time and a lot of mental processing to distill my thoughts and ideas into a simple but comprehensive model, and your feedback and clarifying questions helped turn this into a reality.

To Gerry Dimova, my copywriter, who has a phenomenal way with words. Thank you for taking the time to get to know my audience, interpreting my messy notes about what each part of the model should contain, and then helping me to come up with the word BRAVE and the subheadings for each part.

To my KPI accountability group – Kay Nyenuh, Michael Back and Mat Davis. Thank you for helping me stay on task and actually get the words onto the pages.

To Cathy Love – thank you for coaching me through the process of finishing the book, and then getting it out there into the world. Thank you also for the suggestion of *Braver Than You Think* as a title.

To the team at Michael Hanrahan Publishing. Michael and Anna – thank you for guiding me through the publishing process, with clear markers, reminders and support to help me know what to expect. Charlotte – thank you for understanding my audience and

Acknowledgements

purpose, and supporting me with the editing. Peter – thank you for your extraordinary patience with designing my book cover.

To my fellow Physiotherapists, Occupational Therapists and Speech Pathologists who I have had the privilege of working with or learning from – in particular, Judy Willey, Anna Deguara, Sian Neubecker, Penny Ireland and Katy Caynes – thank you for making me a better and more well-rounded therapist.

To my team at Move and Play – Anna, Rachael, Zora, Sammy, Natalia and Kathleen. Thank you for continuing to passionately support the children and families we work with while I have been busy behind the scenes writing this book and developing our service to better care for our clients.

To the children, parents and families I have worked with over my career, whether it be through my clinical work, my research, or now as a business owner. Thank you for sharing your stories so honestly and bravely and allowing me and other therapists to be a part of your lives. We, as therapists, learn so much from each of you.

Finally, a very special thanks to my husband Steve, and to my kids Isabelle and Oscar. Steve, thank you for always supporting me and for looking after the kids on many weekends so I could focus my attention on writing and editing. And to Issy and Oscar, thank you for helping me to understand what it means to be a parent. You all mean the world to me.

First published in 2019 by Emily Hayles

© Emily Hayles 2019

The moral rights of the author have been asserted

All rights reserved. Except as permitted under the *Australian Copyright Act 1968* (for example, a fair dealing for the purposes of study, research, criticism or review), no part of this book may be reproduced, stored in a retrieval system, communicated or transmitted in any form or by any means without prior written permission.

All inquiries should be made to the author.

A catalogue entry for this book is available from the National Library of Australia.

ISBN: 978-1-925921-14-4

Project management and text design by Michael Hanrahan Publishing
Cover design by Peter Reardon

Disclaimer

The material in this publication is of the nature of general comment only, and does not represent professional advice. It is not intended to provide specific guidance for particular circumstances and it should not be relied on as the basis for any decision to take action or not take action on any matter which it covers. Readers should obtain professional advice where appropriate, before making any such decision. To the maximum extent permitted by law, the author and publisher disclaim all responsibility and liability to any person, arising directly or indirectly from any person taking or not taking action based on the information in this publication.

Contents

Introduction **1**

Part I: Be aware **13**
1. Understanding early identification and intervention **15**
2. Identifying a developmental issue in your child **27**
3. Receiving a diagnosis and starting early intervention **41**
4. Considering your approach to helping your child **59**
5. Being aware of future difficulties and changes **69**

Part II: Recognise your child's needs **79**
6. The interconnectedness of child development **81**
7. Understanding your child's development **93**
8. Identifying your child's strengths and prioritising needs **111**
9. Getting the help you need **125**

Part III: Assist, but don't insist **141**
10. Looking at what's important **143**
11. Assistive technology and equipment **163**

Part IV: Validate your child **183**
12. Developing self-identity and competence **185**
13. Helping your child connect with others **209**

Part V: Empower yourself and your family 225

14. Working out values and making time for what's important **229**
15. Finding support and choosing your battles **243**

Conclusion: Bringing it all together **253**

Further reading and helpful resources **257**

Appendix A: Common diagnoses **261**
Appendix B: Developmental milestones for children with Down syndrome **265**
Appendix C: Medical service providers **269**
Appendix D: Funding options while accessing treatment **277**

Introduction

Imagine this

You are a parent. You have a beautiful little child who you cherish and love immensely. However, you have this niggling concern about their development. They are just not quite doing what you expect them to. They just don't seem to be doing things the way other babies do, or like their older siblings did. You might have been concerned about their development for some time. Perhaps you were told at the time of your child's birth that the specialists had concerns about their future development, or perhaps you noticed issues yourself in the first few weeks or months of life.

You might just know something is not quite right, something is going on, but you are not sure what. You have asked family and friends about it, but no-one seems to know any better than you. You took your child to your family doctor and they weren't sure either, so they referred your child to see a paediatrician. You had to wait for a while for the paediatrician's appointment (they are all booked out for many weeks in advance) so, in the meantime, you consulted with 'Dr Google' about your concerns about your child, but you are not sure which information you should trust. You delight in each thing your child does that shows they are progressing, but you also worry each time you notice they are finding something difficult. Each day, as you wait for the paediatrician's appointment, you get a little more anxious about what the paediatrician might say, but you are also hopeful that the paediatrician will finally give you some clarity about what is going on for your child and how you can help.

The day of the paediatrician's appointment has arrived. You and your partner wait patiently with your child in the waiting room.

They call you in. The paediatrician is friendly and kind, and asks you lots of questions. They examine your child. They might recommend your child has some more tests. Or they might be able to give you some information straightaway. Regardless, at some point the paediatrician tells you that your child has, or most likely has, a disability or special needs …

It feels like time stands still when you receive the diagnosis. The paediatrician speaks with you about what this means for your child. They answer your questions as best they can – some they can answer, some they cannot. You may struggle to comprehend it. You may feel a sense of relief that you finally have some answers. You may feel sad, or anxious, or grateful for some answers and information. It might be hard for you to imagine what this means for your child – and how it contrasts with how you imaged your child's life as they grow up.

Maybe you have a great discussion with the paediatrician; maybe not. Maybe you feel okay at the appointment, but you have multiple questions afterwards. The paediatrician has given you a couple of information sheets about your child's condition, and the funding and services available for your child and family. They've also said they will refer your child to some therapists who can help.

You look down at your child, and your heart and head are filled with a mix of love, grief, concern, and uncertainty. But you also feel a sense of relief and hope because at least now you can start taking some steps to help your child to be the best they can be. But what steps? Taking you through these next steps is what this book is all about.

Who this book is for

This book is designed to help parents of children with disabilities or special needs understand how they can help their child to lead their best life, where they are as happy, healthy and connected as they can be – regardless of their diagnosis or condition.

When your child is first diagnosed, you likely have three key worries.

Introduction

You're not sure what to expect

Every parent who has a child with a developmental concern or disability worries about their child's future. And much of the worry stems from uncertainty. The somewhat predictable life you had previously envisaged for your child has changed, and now you are feeling uncertain, unsure and unprepared.

You still have lots of questions about your child's future. What do you do now? Will your child be able to walk? Will they learn to talk? Will they learn to look after themselves? How can I help them? Will they be able to go to a mainstream school? Will they have friends? Will our family be able to cope? And, most importantly, will they be happy?

You don't know how to help

The uncertainty you have about your child's future fuels another uncertainty – how you should help your child? The amount of information and misinformation out there is overwhelming. A myriad of therapy and treatment and support options are also available. How and where can you get information and support that is appropriate for your child? Who can you ask for help? The paperwork seems never-ending and fighting the systems seems like a lost cause.

You want to feel confident that you are doing the right things for your child, confident in your ability to make decisions about your child's care, and confident that you are doing everything you can to help them to be as happy and as healthy as they can be. But, right now, finding the best path for your child and family is challenging and sometimes overwhelming.

You and your family are stretched and stressed

Your life has become a chaos of therapy appointments, paperwork, and coordinating and looking after your child. How do you find a balance between maximising your child's progress and opportunities, and also letting them just be a 'kid'? You may feel under financial and emotional strain. Taking care of yourself and spending quality family time seems truly impossible. How do you juggle everything?

How do you make the time for self-care, family responsibilities, and your child's needs?

The truth is, parenting any child comes with difficulties, but parenting a child with developmental delays, disabilities or special needs comes with additional demands and challenges. As a parent, you need and want all the courage and support you can gather.

If these problems feel all too familiar, this book is for you. This book is for parents who are looking for a guide on how to help their child to live the best life possible, and who want to invest and prepare for their child's future.

Why I wrote this book

In my professional life, I am a physiotherapist who has worked with children and families my whole career. I have met and worked with hundreds of parents of children with developmental delays and disabilities. I have spent countless hours listening to parents' stories and experiences, learning about their aspirations for their children, the difficulties they face, as well as the joy, hope, frustrations and fears they experience. Over the years, I have noticed that many different parents share similar stories; the difficulties they experience are shared, and their journeys are similar. As a result, I have also found myself repeating the same information, guiding parents using similar principles and similar approaches to help them to support their child the best they can.

I firmly believe that you, the parent, know your child better than anyone else. You spend the most time with your child, watching, playing with and caring for them. You are also the person who loves and devotes themselves the most to your child. And you have the most impact on your child's life. My role, as with all the health professionals you work with, is merely to provide guidance and direction to help you help your child.

So who else better to empower with knowledge and information on how to help their child to develop than you? Disappointingly, I've found very few books available for parents of children with disabilities (yet hundreds of books are available for teachers!). And although a mountain of information is available for parents on the internet about child development as well as countless blogs and websites with information about supporting children with developmental issues and disabilities, parents of children with disability are already stretched in the time they have available to them – so trying to sort through this mountain to find what is relevant, useful, reputable and appropriate is a daunting and time-consuming task. Parents want to start helping their children as soon as possible, and don't have time to sort through this amount of information to find the gems of wisdom that will help their child.

And so, I decided to write this book – so that parents could have a resource available to them that can help them help their child. This book is not designed to provide you guidance on the specific therapies or interventions your child needs. Instead, it provides you with the foundation of information that will allow you to understand your child's overall needs better, help you to make decisions about your child's care, and help you, your child and your family to lead a happy and fulfilling life.

Confidence comes through knowledge

In my personal life, I am the mum of two small children. Although my children do not have a disability, I do understand a parent's desire to do the best I can for my children, and the difficulty of doing so in the busyness of modern family life. I also understand the importance of feeling confident as a parent to be able to make decisions for my children and be able to advocate for their needs.

Let me share an example of this. Of course, in comparison to what parents of children with disabilities have to deal with, this example seems pretty minor, but it does provide an illustration of my personal experiences as a parent and knowing my child best. When my daughter was three years old, I booked her in for her flu vaccination. My daughter has a bright and curious personality, and is not the kind of kid you can trick into something. So I had been preparing her for the vaccination and what I needed her to do. We had rehearsed that her job was to sit very still, Mummy's job was to hold her tight in a big cuddle, and the nurse's job was to put the needle in her arm. We had talked about how it might sting a little bit, and she might cry, but as long as she sat still, she had done her job perfectly. We had also talked about her being able to choose whether she wanted to close her eyes or look at the needle. That was her choice, and she decided she wanted to look. These were all strategies I had learnt from my time working with occupational therapists during procedures in hospital, so I knew what worked best from both a health professional's and a mother's point of view.

When we were in the nurse's office, my daughter was understandably somewhat anxious and was finding it harder to sit still than during our rehearsal sessions. (I must admit I was anxious myself that my preparation with her had made her anxiety worse!) But I repeated what we had practised at home, and we were ready to go. And then the nurse said, 'Now just close your eyes tight' – and that was the moment that my daughter's anxiety became higher, because closing her eyes tight was not what she wanted to do. Thankfully, I knew that I knew my daughter best and what she wanted, so I interrupted the nurse and asked my daughter again, 'Do you want to close your eyes or do you want to watch?' Again she said, 'I want to watch.' I think the nurse was by now a bit anxious that I was the one not coping; however, it was the complete opposite. I knew my child and what she wanted, and because I was empowered with knowledge of what would work, I felt confident enough to speak up. In the end, my daughter got her needle, she watched it as it went in as she wanted to, she cried momentarily – and then giggled shortly afterwards because she said it didn't even hurt.

This small moment is what I want parents to feel most (if not all) of the time – confident in their knowledge of what is best for their child, confident that they are able to make the best decisions for their child, and confident that they are able to speak up and request what is best for their child.

Introduction

How this book is structured

This book is structured to follow the BRAVE model, a model I developed from countless hours of talking with, learning from and supporting families of children with disabilities. During these conversations and interactions, I came to learn from parents that raising a child with a disability involves more than just ensuring your child gets the therapy or care supports they need. However, at least initially, parents can sometimes get caught in a rollercoaster of activity that sees them doing as much as they can for their child, without taking a step back to think about the bigger picture for their child and family.

The BRAVE model provides a framework to help you consider this bigger picture. It is designed to help you understand all the fundamental things that need to be considered when designing a life for your child with a disability and for your family. The model helps you through the process – all the way from identifying, understanding and getting help for your child's developmental concerns, to supporting your child to become as independent as possible and develop their self-identity, to reducing stress and ensuring a more balanced family life. The BRAVE model aims to help you gain the knowledge, courage and resilience that you will need to help your child to live their best life, within the context of their individual needs as well as those of the rest of your family.

The key pillars of the BRAVE model, which form the five parts of this book, are:

- *Be aware (and act early):* The sooner you identify your child's needs and get help, the sooner your child can improve and develop. In the chapters in this part, you will learn about the concepts of 'early identification' and 'early intervention', and why they are so important to maximising your child's long-term outcomes. I outline how to get help as early as possible and make sure your concerns are heard, the difference between a diagnosis and prognosis, and the different treatment options available to you. And finally I cover how early identification and intervention continues throughout your child's childhood to help prevent complications and maximise their outcomes as they grow and change.

- *Recognise your child's needs:* In this part, you will learn about your child's development and how all of your child's needs – physical, communication, self-care, independence, cognitive, social and emotional – are interconnected. I share with you some models that can help you to understand your child's unique developmental needs in all areas of their life. You will also learn how to prioritise your child's needs, set goals or focus areas for your child's treatment, and how to find people or services that can help you and your child.

- *Assist but don't insist:* As soon as you can understand your child's unique needs, you are ready to start helping them grow into an independent individual. In the chapters in this part, you'll find out more about what is important when fostering your child's independence, including choosing the right challenges, the importance of variety and repetition, and optimising their posture and positioning. I also look at embracing assistive technology, and finding the best equipment to help your child become as self-reliant and confident as possible.

- *Validate your child:* Independence goes hand in hand with a healthy self-image. In this part, you will learn how to empower your child to develop a strong sense of who they are – based on their skills, passions, relationships, and participation, rather than on their disability. I delve into the concepts of presuming competence, following your child's lead, helping your child to develop resilience, and finding the balance between therapies and just letting your child be a child who is able to follow their passions, and to participate in life the way they choose.

- *Empower yourself:* The final part is about empowering yourself, as a parent and as a family. The importance of this to your child's life cannot be underestimated. Giving yourself time to rest and recharge will help you be a better parent and take

Introduction

better care of your child. In this part, you will learn how to ensure you are taking care of yourself and your family, how to develop connections with other parents and families, and ways to balance your child's needs with the needs of all other members of your family. In addition, I share with you strategies you can use to advocate for your child's needs, without burning yourself or your family out.

The five parts of this book reflect the five areas that parents like you need to consider and understand when helping your child to develop the best they can, and ultimately lead a happy and fulfilling life. The BRAVE model could be applied to any child, regardless of whether they have a disability or not; however, this book specifically applies the model for children with developmental delays or disabilities. Throughout the chapters of this book, I use case examples to help illustrate how the principles of the BRAVE model apply for children with specific needs. The cases include children with cerebral palsy, Down syndrome, autism, rare genetic disorders, sensory needs, and intellectual impairment. However, I want to assure you that, even if your child's condition or diagnosis is not listed in the previous sentence, the BRAVE framework and the principles that make up the BRAVE framework are still very much worth considering and applying for your child.

The parts of the model and the book have been placed in order of B-R-A-V-E because they follow the learning process that parents go through when their child is initially diagnosed with a developmental delay or disability. So when first reading the book, or if your child has only recently been diagnosed, it might be a good idea to read the chapters in the order they have been written. However, no single part of the model needs to be 'completed' before the next, and throughout your parenting journey you might need to draw knowledge from different sections at different times. So later on down the track, or if your child is a bit older, you may prefer to pick and choose which chapter or part is most relevant to you at any period of time, or go back to different sections depending on your child's needs in that moment. However, ultimately, it is important to understand that each of the five parts contributes equally to you being able to help your child lead a life that is as happy, healthy and fulfilling as possible. No one part is more important than the other.

Throughout the book, I will use examples, exercises, case studies and quotes to help you understand and draw from my and other parents' experiences. You will also find at the end of the book a 'Further reading' section, which provides a list of useful references, including those I have used when developing this book, so you can explore more information about a specific topic.

My hope for you ...

I get no greater joy and satisfaction as a physiotherapist than to see the children I work with achieve things they can be proud of. I am also very grateful that I have been privileged enough to have many families share these exciting moments with me. Perhaps my favourite story is of a little guy – let's call him Sean (all names have been changed for the examples used through this book) – who has cerebral palsy. I had seen Sean since he was about 18 months old, and we had been working with him for many years to help him to learn to walk. Sean was able to walk around with a walker by himself but, as always, Sean, his parents, and I were quietly hoping that maybe he would learn to take some steps independently. Three years later, I received a phone call on a Monday from the grandma of this little boy – calling me to say that Sean had taken six steps independently on the previous Friday afternoon. When it happened, his whole family cried because they were so excited. His mum was in Townsville at the time (400 km from our home town of Mackay) with her second son who needed to be in hospital for a few weeks after birth. When Sean's mum received the phone call on the Friday afternoon, she was so excited she cried and then got in the car and drove all the way back to Mackay that evening to see Sean walking on his own. I welled up as the family told me this story, and when I finally got to see him walk for myself. (And I am welling up now writing it!) This is why I do what I do.

Introduction

My hope is that by sharing the information contained in this book, I can help more parents develop confidence that they are doing the best they can for their child, and experience the joy of seeing their child achieve great things and lead happy and fulfilling lives.

Part I: Be aware (and act early)

Seeing a child develop is pretty amazing. In a very short time, only a couple of years, most typically developing children will go from tiny, defenceless and totally dependent little babies to walking, talking, climbing, sometimes back-chatting, but mostly lovely little people who are (hopefully) well on their way to developing into a well-functioning human being.

Then, after the early years, children just keep on growing, developing and changing at a seemingly fast rate. In the schooling years, children continue to go through rapid growth and learning, experiencing changes in the way their body is shaped, as well as hormonal and cognitive changes, all which affect how they move and how they interact and get on in the world.

The rapid developmental changes that we see on the outside reflect even bigger developmental changes that are occurring in your child's brain, as well as in their muscles, joints, and sensory systems.

Because children develop, grow and change so rapidly and constantly, it is important for parents to be aware of any difficulties their child might be having and seek help for that as early as possible. Problems that are missed or ignored or denied, although perhaps minor when first noticed, can become bigger problems as your child grows and develops, and can have far-reaching impacts – more than perhaps imagined when they were first noticed.

As you can see, childhood, and particularly early childhood, is a naturally occurring period of rapid development for all children, regardless of whether they have a disability or not. Early intervention aims to harness this period of rapid growth and development, and brings about the most change and improvement possible at a time when their body is naturally primed for change and improvement. The sooner you identify the difficulties your child is experiencing, and hopefully figure out the underlying cause for those difficulties, the sooner you can start treatment. In the chapters in this part, you will learn about the concepts of early identification and early intervention, as they relate to when you first notice concerns about your child's development, and also as they relate to being aware and acting on changes and concerns as your child grows and develops. In addition, you will discover how to get your concerns heard, the difference between a diagnosis and prognosis, and how you might be able to anticipate your child's and family's future.

CHAPTER ONE

Understanding early identification and intervention

Early identification and intervention is what it says it is – picking up on developmental issues early, and treating them as early as possible. The purpose of early identification and intervention is to try and identify and treat any health or developmental issues in a child early, in an attempt to prevent them from becoming a long-term issue, so the child can achieve the best progress and developmental outcome possible.

Did you ever take your child to a baby screening check, like a hearing check? Or an annual developmental review with your GP? Or a pre-school health check? All of these programs are screening programs that aim to identify children who might be having developmental issues so that they can get started on treatment as early as possible.

Benefits of identifying and treating developmental difficulties early

The importance of identifying and treating developmental difficulties early all comes down to four things: neuroplasticity, habits, the flow-on effect of developmental delays, and growth-related changes.

Neuroplasticity

Neuroplasticity is the ability of the brain to change and adapt. Many years ago it was thought that the brain was a static organ and could not change – it was thought, for example, that if a person had an injured brain, that was permanent, and nothing could be done to help the brain to heal the damage. Nowadays, it is very well understood that the brain can and does change, adapt and, in some cases, recover in response to the input or stimuli it receives (See the 'Further reading' section at the end of this book for some great resources by Norman Doidge and Karen Pape on this topic.) And the brain can change in many ways. Different areas of the brain can adapt to take over control of functions they normally wouldn't. Connections between cells in the brain that allow messages to be passed from the brain to the body can strengthen or weaken over time in response to use or disuse. The proportion of grey matter (the part of the brain that is responsible for interpreting information and creating messages to go out to the body) can also change over time, becoming more or less active, or physically getting larger or shrinking.

All of these changes occur in response to the input the brain receives. For example, if you decide to start playing a musical instrument such as a violin, through practice and repetition, you will get better at playing the violin because your brain and your body will adapt. The areas of your brain responsible for moving your fingers, reading music and hearing whether you are on key or not will become more active, and the connections in these areas of the brain will become stronger. These changes allow for you and your body to become more effective and efficient at playing the violin. The input your brain receives helps the brain to adapt, which then helps you to play the violin better.

Neuroplasticity and children

So how does neuroplasticity relate to brain development and children? Let's look at some examples. In a study by Sterling et al. (see the 'Further reading' for full details), MRI scans of children with hemiplegic cerebral palsy (where one side of their body has movement and sensory differences due to damage on one side of their brain) have shown their brains can adapt following a period of intensive therapy, demonstrating increased grey matter (brain cells) as well as motor improvements in their hand use. Conversely, another renowned study by Sheridan et al. of children who lived in Romanian orphanages and experienced neglect as a result of less stimulus and human connection compared to other children their age showed that the brains of these children were smaller with fewer connections between different parts of their brains compared to other children their age. As you can see, the brain adapts to both positive stimuli (such as an enriching environment, interactions with others, activities and therapy) and negative stimuli (such as unstimulating environments, trauma and neglect).

In terms of timing, neuroplasticity is known to be much higher in the developing brain. A developing brain is naturally going through a period of significant adaptation as it lays down new connections between different parts of the brain, strengthens connections, and also decreases connections that are no longer needed. A developing brain has high potential for neuroplasticity and change because it is a highly adaptive and changing organ during this time.

This means the neuroplastic potential of the brain is high in the first few years of a child's life. In this period, millions of neural connections between different neurons in the brain are made in response to the stimuli received. These connections deliver messages between the body and the brain, and create a map or a framework from which the child's body then moves, learns and functions for the rest of their life. It is these pathways that the infant's and then toddler's brain creates that provide the foundation for all of their future learning. If a child does not receive appropriate stimulus in this period, they miss laying down appropriate pathways at a neuronal level. If a child with a movement disorder learns to move using an atypical pattern, for example, that is the pathway that is laid down in their brain at a neuronal level.

Habits

Habits, in a developmental context, refer to the automatic or subconscious ways that someone does something. For example, children who are learning to roll might develop a habit of always rolling to one side – it is not that they cannot roll to the other side, but just that they have practised this method and so find it much more automatic to roll to that preferred side.

For children with developmental difficulties, habits are the ways that we see children move or do things. What might start out as a one-off way of doing something becomes a habitual way as a result of repeated practice, which then lays down and reinforces the pathways in the brain during their early developmental experiences (as discussed in the preceding section). For example, a child with cerebral palsy who learns to walk up on the toes of their left foot, will reinforce and strengthen the neural pathways in the brain that control the action of walking up on the toes of their left foot. Over time, as a result of repeatedly practising and reinforcing this atypical pattern of movement, this pattern becomes an 'ingrained' neural pathway that means the child will automatically move in that way. Another common example is for a child with Down syndrome who learns to move between sitting and lying by moving forwards and doing the splits. As a result of repeatedly practising that movement pattern, they will reinforce and strengthen those neural pathways in the brain, making it harder to change their habitual way of moving in the long term.

Infants and young children are very clever – once they learn to successfully achieve a task using an atypical or inefficient movement pattern, their brain remembers the success of that movement. Because the outcome of attempting that task was successful, the infant or child and will repeat it over and over again, reinforcing those patterns – even though the way they are moving may not be efficient to their long-term progress. Why would your child learn to move another way when they can already achieve that task using another method, even if it is a less effective strategy?

Early intervention aims to help your child to move using optimal or more typical and successful patterns *before* they figure out how to move in other suboptimal patterns, and before the suboptimal movement patterns become habits and strengthened and ingrained in the brain. By receiving early intervention and learning optimal patterns first, these optimal movement patterns can become the habitual way your child ends up moving. In contrast, changing someone's learnt or habitual way of moving can be very difficult.

Case study

Georgia is a little girl with hemiplegic cerebral palsy (see appendix A for an explanation of common diagnoses) who I began seeing when she was approximately eight months old. Georgia had quite a severe hemiplegia, with lots of spasticity and little use of her right arm. When I met Georgia, she was able to sit up by herself, but she was not yet moving on the floor. Georgia was ready to commence the process of learning to crawl, so during therapy we worked on teaching Georgia to be able to lean on and take some weight through her right arm. Despite us working quite consistently on helping Georgia learn to crawl, she soon learnt to 'bottom shuffle' (scoot along the floor in a sitting position by using her good arm to prop herself up as needed and her legs to scoot herself forwards).

For someone who has a hemiplegia, bottom shuffling is a way that they can learn to move around the floor in their environment. However, bottom shuffling did not allow Georgia to take weight through her affected right arm, which meant less opportunity for her to stretch and strengthen that arm. Once Georgia figured out that she could bottom shuffle successfully to get around her environment, it was very difficult for us to convince her to learn to crawl – why would she crawl, which is somewhat difficult due to her right arm being weaker, when she could bottom shuffle to get where she needs to go? We wanted Georgia to crawl to optimise the movement and function in her right arm and leg. But the purpose of crawling is to get from A to B, and Georgia had already learnt how to do that using bottom shuffling. In the end, Georgia did learn to crawl. However, she would almost always choose to bottom shuffle to get around the floor, as a result it being a more automatic movement pattern from her repeatedly practising that movement pattern and reinforcing those pathways in her brain.

Flow-on effect of developmental delays

A developmental concern in one area almost never has just a single isolated impact. Instead, it will almost always have a much wider reach, affecting other areas of a child's development and potentially their growth. In part II, I explain the importance of recognising the breadth of your child's needs, and the breadth of the impact of their developmental concerns in more detail, but to set the context for you now, I will explain one example here.

For children who are not able to sit with good posture, whether it is for physical or sensory reasons, this difficulty has far-reaching consequences than just 'not being able to sit with good posture'. A child continuing to sit in a suboptimal posture can potentially affect one or all of the following areas of the child's development:

- The child's posture will affect the position of their head, which can affect how well they can use their eyes and how well they can turn their head, and predisposes them to potentially experiencing muscle, joint or nerve pain in their neck, shoulders, back and hips.

- The child's posture will affect how well they can use their hands. If their trunk posture affects where and how well they can position and hold their arms, this will have an impact on how well they can write, use scissors, use cutlery, fasten buttons and complete other fine motor tasks.

- The child's posture will affect their attention and concentration. If their sitting posture makes it harder for the child to sit still for a longer period (either due to discomfort, poor body awareness and feedback, or fast fatigue), the child will not be able to concentrate and attend to activities such as mealtimes, school work and homework. This will have an impact on their ability to learn and to engage in social activities with their family and friends, and they may appear to have behavioural difficulties, even if they don't.

As you can see, if we can optimise the child's posture as soon as possible through early intervention, these flow-on effects and difficulties can be avoided or minimised. This same principle applies across all areas of development: if you can help your child learn to move, their problem solving and social skills will be enhanced; if you can help your child learn to communicate, their behaviour and social skills will be enhanced; if you can help your child learn to use their hands to point or sign, their communication skills and choice-making skills will be enhanced. Every part of your child's development has a flow-on effect to other areas, so it is important to identify any challenges or difficulties with development early so that you can minimise these effects.

Growth-related changes

The tricky thing about kids is their bodies are constantly growing. And when children grow, their bodies are constantly adapting. Their bones change shape, and the alignment and thickness of their bones also change. Their muscles grow, lengthen and strengthen, or learn to fire more quickly or slowly. Their overall body shape changes and, as a result, the way they move and interact with the world also changes and adapts.

Some of the adaptions due to growth within your child's body are due to natural or inherent bony changes that occur in all children. For example, all children are typically born with slightly bowed legs that become straighter over time. However, many growth changes that occur in your child's body occur as a result of what your child does. For example, changes can be affected by:

- the weight or load going through your child's body parts, including the impact of gravity and their body weight
- the type and variety of activities your child does
- the postures that your child adopts, especially postures that are sustained over time.

For children who are typically developing, most of the bone and muscle adaptations that occur throughout childhood allow the bones to become stronger, the muscles to become more effective and efficient at moving our body parts, and both of these contribute to improvements or maturation of developmental skills. For example, the hip bones of toddlers are not fully developed, and are in a less stable position than adult hips. As they grow and develop, children's hip bones typically get stronger, their hip joint becomes deeper, the ligaments at the front of the hip lengthen, and the alignment of their hip bones changes. All these changes make their hip joint more stable, and put it in a more efficient position for walking and running. Importantly, these changes in the hip joint rely on the child taking weight through their legs, and moving their legs in typical patterns. However, for children with developmental delays and disabilities, whose movement patterns, physical activities and postures might not follow that of a typically developing child, the growth changes in the bones and muscles might not be as optimal, or they could be detrimental to the child's postures or movement skills.

Continuing the example of hip development, the hip bones and the hip socket rely on the weight of the body going down through them to form the deep ball and socket shape that normally makes the hip joint so stable in adults. But for children with developmental disabilities who do not do as much standing as usually expected, their hip bones and sockets do not have weight going through them, which means they don't form deep sockets and, therefore, their hips are more likely to move out of the socket, putting them at risk of hip migration and dislocation, which can potentially cause pain. This is why therapists routinely recommend all children with cerebral palsy, and children with other conditions that cause delays in their standing and walking ability, to use a standing frame – to help them to start taking weight through their legs so their hip sockets can start to develop. They are also likely to recommend follow-up hip X-rays and assessments, to try to identify as early as possible if their hips are moving out of their sockets – because it is much easier to correct this before the hip has moved out of the socket compared to after.

Case study

Children who are born with hemiplegic cerebral palsy (such as Georgia from the earlier case study in this chapter) will have one side of their body affected. Their arm and leg on one side of their body may have muscles that are weak and stiff and, as a result, they won't use that arm and leg in the same way as they do the other side. With their leg, they won't put as much weight through it, they might stand on it less frequently or for less time than the other side, and they might move it differently when crawling, standing and walking. The impact of all of these differences is that the bones of that leg may not grow as much as the bones in the other leg, and so many children with hemiplegia will end up having one leg that is shorter than the other. Each time the child grows, the difference in their leg length may change. It is important that this difference in leg length, and any ongoing changes in the difference in leg length, are identified early and addressed. Putting a wedge or a deeper sole on the leg that is shorter, for example, will encourage the child to bear their weight more evenly through both legs. As a result, the child's bones are more likely to then grow more evenly too.

What is the ideal timing of early intervention?

Simply put, the best time for early intervention is as early as possible.

As discussed earlier in this chapter, research has shown that infant brains, especially between birth and two years of age, go through a rapid period of development as neural pathways are laid down and reinforced. Over this time period, children typically learn an enormous number of fundamental skills that set them up to be able to develop higher level skills in the future.

From a motor perspective, these skills include the ability to hold their head up, roll, sit up by themselves, crawl, stand, walk, run, climb, jump, and to use their hands to reach, grasp, release and manipulate objects, and to use their hands together. These fundamental movement skills allow them to move around their environment, move up and down in their environment, and explore their environment. From a communication point of view, in the first two years of life, children learn to communicate through eye contact, sounds, gestures and, eventually, words and basic sentences. From a social point of view, they also learn to develop a sense of themselves, of who they are separate to their primary carers, and develop strong relationships with others. And from a cognitive point of view, children discover and learn things through cause and effect, imitation, develop early problem solving skills, and about boundaries.

As you can see, the first few years of life are a very developmentally rich time, with a lot of changes and progress occurring. As a result, early intervention should ideally happen as early as possible in your child's life to help ensure they can learn as many of these fundamental skills as possible, using optimal patterns, which will set them up for being able to continue to develop their higher level skills in the future.

For children whose developmental difficulties are not identified during the first two years of life, the timing of early intervention should still optimally be as soon as possible after the child's difficulties are identified. So if, for example, you notice your child is having difficulty with communication and interacting with others at the age of three, getting help and starting early intervention for that as soon as possible is ideal. You may be tempted to hold off on getting an assessment or seeking help for their child because you're not sure if it is anything to worry about, you don't want to be seen to be an anxious parent worrying about something they don't need to, or you're not quite ready to admit that there might be something different about your child. I talk about this in more detail in the next chapter, but for now I want to encourage you to seek help as soon as possible, regardless of these concerns. The best-case scenario is that the assessment will show that they are developing within normal limits and you can be reassured and rest easy knowing that everything is okay. And the worst-case scenario is that there might be something your child is having difficulties with and you start getting help for that – which, in my view, is a positive outcome anyway.

CHAPTER TWO

Identifying a developmental issue in your child

Parents know their child better than anyone else. In my experience, parents often know their child is not developing as expected before they seek the help of a doctor or other health professional. As a result, I think it is important that parents are empowered with the knowledge and strategies to make sure they can identify concerns with their child's development and get help as quickly as they need to.

If you are reading this book, I expect that you either already know that your child has a developmental concern and have seen someone about it (for example, you might have already got a diagnosis or started therapy and supports for your child), or you have concerns about your child's development, but you have not yet sought diagnosis or help. Regardless of which category you fit into, I want to assure you that the large majority of health professionals will take you seriously when you share your concerns.

This chapter is all about ensuring you, as a parent, are aware of the signs your child might have a developmental concern. But, more importantly, it also provides the knowledge and the confidence for you to know how to get help for your child as soon as possible – even if you doubt whether your concerns are warranted, and even if you don't feel like others (perhaps friends and family, or even the first health professional you took your child to) have listened to you. If you read the previous chapter, you know how important it is to get help early for your child, so this chapter is about making sure you can get help when you need it.

Signs your child has a developmental issue

You don't need to be a health professional to be able to identify if your child has a developmental issue. As a parent, you spend more time with your child than anyone else. This means that you understand better than anyone else what your child can and can't do, and how your child's abilities and behaviours might vary depending on factors such as the time of day, the environment and the people around them (to name just a few). You have also seen changes in your child over time, so you know whether these potential developmental concerns have gotten better, worse, or remained the same over time. All of this knowledge of your child is very relevant and valuable, and you should not underestimate your insight just because you 'are not a health professional', 'are just a mum', or 'this is my first child, so I don't really know what to expect'.

To help you understand how important your knowledge of your child is, and the validity of your concerns, here's how I, as a health professional, approach the initial assessment process. When I first meet a child and a family, I usually see them for one to two hours for their initial assessment. In that assessment, I want to do my best to understand the concerns you have for your child, and to assess your child to see what might be contributing to their developmental delays or difficulties. As the parent, you have spent weeks, months or years (depending on your child's age when you first come to see me) getting to know your child, observing their strengths, weaknesses

Identifying a developmental issue in your child

and behaviours, and how these have changed over time. You have far more understanding of your child than I do, so I rely heavily on your descriptions of your child's abilities and behaviours to gauge whether or not what I am seeing within our session matches what you are describing. I want these descriptions not to challenge what you're saying, but to determine if what I am seeing is an accurate reflection of how your child actually is. So, for me and all health professionals you come in contact with, your knowledge of your child is vital, right from the initial assessment.

If you are not sure whether what you are seeing in your child should be cause for concern, the following outlines some signs that your child might have a developmental concern that you should seek a review and help for. However, please note that developmental signs can be many and varied, so this list is not exhaustive. If you review this list and the concerns you have for your child do not fit into this list, I would encourage you to still seek an assessment and help from a health professional or therapist.

Signs to look out for in early infancy or early development:

- Your baby feels floppy or stiff to hold, or they hold their limbs very stiffly.

- Your baby does not use their eyes or vision as expected (not looking at things in their environment), or they are not interacting with you as you would expect them to (making eye contact, cooing or babbling, interacting or exploring toys and other things in their environment).

- You have concerns about how your baby is learning to move, or they are delayed in their movement skills; for example, they are not rolling or sitting or standing around the age when they would be expected to.

- Your baby uses one side of their body more than the other side (for example, reaching with one arm but not the other; kicking one leg much more than the other).

- Your baby was born prematurely, and has experienced medical events that put them at risk of a developmental concern (such as a bleed on their brain, or an early infection).
- Your baby has been diagnosed with a condition that is likely to affect their development. Examples of conditions that can be diagnosed early in life include Down syndrome, cerebral palsy, congenital physical conditions such as any form of short stature or limb deficiency and spina bifida.

Signs to look for in later childhood:

- You have concerns about your child's motor skills, such as the way they walk, run, jump, hop, catch a ball and/or climb. They might have poor posture, frequent trips or falls, poor balance and/or coordination. They might appear to move differently from other children and may have trouble keeping up with their peers in games, or they might not be able to do certain activities at all.
- Your child might be taking longer or struggling to learn self-care skills such as toileting, eating and drinking and mealtime behaviours, and washing and dressing.
- Your child might be struggling to keep up with their school work, or is falling behind their classmates. Their handwriting might be messy, or they might have trouble following the teacher's instructions or maintaining focus on class activities.
- Your child does not interact with other people or things in their environment as you would expect them to. For example, your child does not make eye contact, they do not respond to their name.
- Your child is not talking or communicating (including non-verbal interactions) like other children their age.
- Your child has difficulty maintaining attention, gets distracted easily, or has trouble concentrating at home or at school.

- Your child has difficulty managing their emotions or behaviours, and may become unexpectedly overwhelmed in certain situations.
- Your child has been diagnosed with a developmental condition that can be identified later in childhood such as autism spectrum disorder, intellectual impairments or rare genetic conditions, or has acquired a developmental condition due to trauma.

As already mentioned, this list is not exhaustive, and the descriptors are pretty general, so if you have a concern relating to your child that is not on this list, please still seek help for it as early as you can. Even if it turns out you have nothing to worry about, seeking help from a health professional as early as possible will either:

- provide an early baseline assessment that, when combined with later assessments, might help to figure out if something is going on for your child
- provide the peace of mind you need.

I also understand the reassurance early assessment can provide on a personal level. I have a daughter who is four, and a son who is two (at the time of writing). My daughter was an early and very proficient talker – at the age of 18 months she had a pretty big vocabulary for her age, and was putting two to three words together. In comparison, my son is definitely on the slower end of learning to talk. At 18 months, although he had some utterances, he was not actually saying any words. I thought he could understand what I was saying to him, but he was not really saying much that I could understand. So, at the age of 18 months, I took my son to, firstly, an audiologist to see if he could hear adequately, and then to a speech and language pathologist to have his language and speech assessed. While he doesn't have any sort of diagnosis at this stage (and you never know; he may surprise me and end up just learning to talk clearly in the near future), I am at least reassured and confident that I am doing what I can to assist his development of language in these early years, and that I am already 'in the system' should he end up having a diagnosis of some sort.

Achieving milestones – what is important?

If you look up developmental checklists online or in books, or if you take your child for a general developmental check-up, a lot of importance can be placed on their age in relation to achieving certain milestones. For example, a child is typically expected to learn to take their first steps independently at around 12 months of age. However, this is just a 'ballpark' age, and what's considered 'within normal limits' for a child to reach this developmental milestone is actually a wide range. Some children will take their first independent steps at nine months of age; others will take their first independent steps at 18 months of age. Either of these ages can be considered within the 'normal' or 'typical' range for children to start walking independently (in fact, my own children took their first independent steps at 16 months and 18 months of age, despite their mother being a physio!). However, what is more important to understanding about whether your child is developing as expected is *how* they develop – whether they are using typical movement patterns, understanding and starting to use language as expected, and exploring and playing as expected, as well as how they are progressing over time.

When self-assessing your child's development over time, consider the following questions:

- Is your child achieving developmental milestones within the age brackets that they are expected?

- How is your child achieving those milestones? Are they moving or learning as you would expect them to? Or are they doing something unusual that is not typically expected?

- Is your child progressing in development over time? Are they progressing at a rate as expected, or are they falling further and further behind?

This timeline of progress and the information about *how* your child is developing provides a health professional with so much more information about your child's development than whether or not they are achieving a milestone at a specific age (such as whether they sat up by themselves at six months of age). Even more importantly, this timeline of progress and information about developmental patterns also provides much more information about your child's ability to, with the help of some developmental supports, learn and develop over time. (For more on the importance of focusing on the how rather than the when, see chapter 4.)

Avoiding delays

As already discussed, my experience has been that parents are usually the first people to notice that their child is not quite developing as expected, and have usually noticed these differences or difficulties before they book their child in to see a therapist, paediatrician or their GP. However, sometimes parents delay getting an assessment, or can experience delays in actually starting early intervention treatment. These delays can happen for a variety of reasons:

- You might delay seeing a doctor or a therapist because you think that maybe nothing is wrong with your child, or you might be wrong or just worrying over nothing.

- You might have friends and family who have told you not to worry, along with something like, 'my son/brother/grandson/nephew/neighbour didn't sit by himself until he was nine months old and he turned out alright' so you hold off a little longer on seeking help.

- Admitting that your child might have a developmental problem is hard, and you're scared or anxious to know what these difficulties might mean for your child long term.

- Perhaps you have gone to see someone about your child's difficulties, but your concerns were dismissed by the health professional, or you were told it is nothing to worry about. This could have been because the delays in your child's development were reasonably minor to start with and within normal limits; the health professional did not hear or understand what you said or did not observe your child's difficulties within the first session or two; or because you've had trouble explaining or sharing information to enable the heath professional to understand your child's difficulties and the impact on their functioning.

- Perhaps your child was identified as being at risk of developmental delays (for example, as a result of being born prematurely or with a heart condition) and so is already being followed closely or reviewed regularly. However, sometimes these reviews are quite spread out (such as annual reviews), and so developmental difficulties that come up in between appointments might not get reviewed until the child's next routine appointment.
- Your child's developmental difficulty might have been identified, but had been diagnosed as not significant, and so you or even your health professionals have decided to 'watch and wait' – you recognise concerns are there, but that these concerns might just be a variation of normal, so you've decided your child needs a little more time and will likely catch up with their development in the future.
- Finally, your family's life might just be super busy, so getting help from a health professional has been delayed because it is hard to fit everything in.

Very occasionally, a parent has no idea that their child has developmental concerns, and so these concerns are not identified until a routine or unrelated visit to the local doctor or child health nurse; in my experience, however (and as already noted), that situation is reasonably uncommon.

Regardless of the reason, if your child does have developmental difficulties, delaying getting started on therapy and finding help for your child may impact on their overall developmental progress, as well as impact on other areas of their growth and development (as discussed in chapter 1).

The next section covers the practical strategies about how to book in and prepare for that first appointment. However, some parents still lack the confidence to take that next step of actually booking that appointment for their child. If this is you, here are two important things I want you to remind yourself of about seeking help early, which might help you overcome any fear or doubt you have in your mind about taking the next step:

- You DO know your child better than anyone else. Even if this is your first child, even if you don't really think you know anything about child development, even if other friends/relatives/Dr Google are telling you not to worry… YOU know your child better than anyone else. You know what your child can do, what they can't do, what they like and dislike, and how they have grown and changed over time. All of this information is very important and gives you an excellent understanding of your child's unique developmental picture and progress.

- Seeking an opinion or help for your child's possible developmental difficulties early creates no 'bad outcomes'. The worst-case scenario is that your child does have a diagnosed condition that is lifelong – but the very positive silver lining to this is that you can now get help for your child from as early as possible to give them the best chance of achieving their full potential. And the best-case scenarios are either your child is doing fine and you can be reassured they are okay, or your child has a developmental difficulty that can be improved or managed with some early intervention to help them catch up or keep up with their peers. For all of these examples, by seeking help as early as possible, the outcome for your child is the same – you are facilitating them being given the best chance of reaching their full potential, whatever that full potential happens to be.

How to seek help early

As we have discussed so far in this chapter, if you are concerned about your child's development, it is best to seek help as early as possible. However, *how* should you actually go about seeking help for your child?

Depending on what your concerns are for your child, you may choose to book in with a doctor or a therapist, or even both. Booking in with a GP or a paediatrician is useful to get an overall assessment of your child's development. Seeing a GP or paediatrician is also necessary if you think your child might need to have any specific investigations done such as blood tests or X-rays or, alternatively, if you need a referral to see a specialist. (In Australia, to see a specialist such as a neurologist or geneticist, you first need to be referred by a GP or paediatrician.) Seeing a GP or paediatrician will help you commence the process of finding out what might be underlying or causing the difficulties your child is experiencing, which is definitely an important thing to undertake (especially if your child's developmental difficulties are due to an underlying medical condition!).

Sometimes a paediatrician or GP will refer a child to see a therapist to ask for the therapist's opinion on the child's development or presentation so they have more specific information before giving a diagnosis. Alternatively, a therapist, as a result of their specific training in their field of child development, may be able to identify if a child has a developmental difficulty or specific condition prior to the child seeing a paediatrician or other medical specialist. Either way, in terms of starting treatment or intervention for your child's developmental difficulties, while GPs and paediatricians can prescribe medication and provide general advice or strategies, seeing a therapist is also worthwhile. They can provide you with specific help in regards to your child's developmental difficulties.

Therapists such as physios, occupational therapists, and speech and language pathologists, especially those of us who work in the field of child development, have an excellent understanding of the areas affecting your child within the field in which we work. But, even more importantly for your child, therapists have extensive training in the management and treatment of developmental conditions. For example, physiotherapists have specific knowledge and skills in understanding, and helping children to learn how to move. Occupational therapists have specific knowledge and skills in understanding how children look after themselves, relate to and

Identifying a developmental issue in your child

interact with others, and play and think, and can support children to develop these skills. And speech and language pathologists have specific knowledge and skills in understanding how to support children to communicate and eat.

By seeing a therapist as early as possible, even before or at the same time as seeing a GP or paediatrician, you can receive a specific assessment of your child's abilities, which will help the GP or paediatrician achieve a complete and thorough picture of your child's presentation. Not only that, but you will also be able to start on specific treatment to assist your child to improve or maximise those abilities. Most healthcare professionals work with you as part of a team to collate all the relevant information about your child.

At this point, I also want to highly recommend you find experts you can trust, rather than listening to friends or 'Dr Google'. As I mentioned before, well-meaning friends and family might suggest watching and waiting, or tell you stories of children who ended up fine in the end. And if you search for information with 'Dr Google', you are going to find both the worst- and best-case scenarios – neither of which are going to help you or your child. So, instead, find an expert in child development – whether that be a GP, a paediatrician or a therapist – and ask them for help.

My top tips to prepare you for seeking help are as follows:

- Create a diary of your child's current and past developmental progress. Go back through the photos and videos on your phone, review your child's baby books and any personal diaries you have to create a record of your child's development, their progress or changes over time, and any concerns you have had over time. This helps you provide a clear history to the health professional when you are talking to them, which can help them to better understand your concerns and develop a picture of your child over time.

- If your child's developmental concerns or behaviours only occur sometimes or in some situations, try to take videos or photos of these as they occur to bring with you to your first appointment.

- Write down the concerns for your child you want to talk about with the health professional. I suggest you also write down the impact of your child's difficulties on your child's life, what your concerns are for your child's future, and also what outcome you want from the appointment. For example, if your child is not interacting and talking with others as you think they should be, make sure to also explain how that impacts on your child (such as their behaviour is difficult because they get frustrated with not being able to get their point across), and what your concerns are for their future (such as they are starting kindy soon, and you are concerned they are going to be left behind in their early childhood learning). And the outcome you are after might be an assessment and identification of why your child's speech and language is delayed, and/or referral to start therapy to help your child to improve their language. Understanding and being able to articulate this level of information can sometimes help direct the health professional to the action you are ultimately wanting for your child.
- Write down any questions you want to ask the health professional. Sometimes once you are in the appointment, you can get caught up in trying to understand the information the health professional is sharing with you, or your emotions or nervousness can make you forget important things you wanted to discuss. Writing them down means you won't forget anything.
- Consider bringing someone trusted with you to the appointment. Having another person with you can help because they can reiterate what you are saying, they can provide additional examples of the concerns you have for your child, and they can also listen to the information the health professional provides so that they can help you to remember what was said or can discuss the information with your later after the appointment.

Trusting your gut

Although I wish I could say that it never happens, I do know that sometimes parents' concerns can be initially dismissed, or parents are not listened to by the experts they seek help from for their child.

Let me repeat – you know your child better than anyone else. So if you have a lingering concern about your child's development that is not being looked into or has been dismissed by the first person or health professional you see, please trust your gut and seek out further opinions.

Your options for seeking further opinions include:

- Seeing the same health professional again. You can always choose to go back to the same health professional, explain your ongoing concerns and request further investigation or help.

- Seeing another professional with the same position. For example, if you saw a GP the first time, you could seek out the opinion of another GP.

- Seeing another professional with a more specialist position. For example, if you saw a GP the first time, you could seek out the opinion of a paediatrician instead, who has more specialised training in children and childhood conditions.

- Seeing another professional from a different discipline. For example, if you saw a GP or paediatrician the first time (both of whom are doctors or medical professionals), you could seek out the opinion of a paediatric physiotherapist, occupational therapist or speech pathologist. Seeing another professional from a different discipline will help you gather broader information about your child's abilities and difficulties, which can help to form a bigger picture. This can then add to the information the doctor can use to decide what might be going on for your child.

When you seek out the second opinion, make sure you prepare using the same strategies listed in this chapter. But, in addition, explaining to the second health professional why you are seeking their second opinion is also helpful. What about that first opinion did not sit well with you? I know some parents might not want to divulge this information because they do not want to talk badly about another health professional, or they don't want this new health professional to be swayed by the opinions of the previous health professional; however, sharing the information about why the first opinion was not satisfactory to you can help the second health professional better understand areas that might not have been looked into the first time, investigations that have not yet been done, or strategies that have not yet been tried that might help you and your child get to where you want to be sooner.

Whenever you are seeking out the opinions of health professionals, it is so important that you can find people you can trust. These days, a number of diagnoses of childhood developmental conditions or disabilities can happen before any outward signs or symptoms are present. For example, babies can be diagnosed as likely having cerebral palsy from as early as three months of age, before any obvious sign of movement disorder is present (and these diagnostic tests carry reasonably high levels of sensitivity, meaning the outcome is highly likely to be what the assessment tells us it is). Having a health professional or a team of health professionals you trust, who you know are being upfront and honest with you, and are doing everything they can to help you, will help you to recognise the benefits of getting early intervention and help for your child, perhaps even before the signs of their condition or disability are obvious to you.

CHAPTER THREE

Receiving a diagnosis and starting early intervention

Parents can have a whole range of emotions when their child first receives a diagnosis. Some parents are fearful of receiving a diagnosis early in their child's life. They worry that this will pigeonhole their child, that the doctors or allied health team might be wrong with the diagnosis, or that once their child has a diagnosis, or a label, they will never be able to get rid of that diagnosis, even if the doctors are wrong. Maybe their child is just slower than other children, or maybe their child is just doing things a little differently to other children and will end up developing normally. Other parents are relieved to finally have some answers and information, and are ready to get started on helping their child. And others can be overwhelmed – a diagnosis can bring them to a halt, and they need time to process what this means for their child, for them as parents and for their family. Ultimately, receiving a diagnosis can be a momentous and variable experience. A diagnosis can mean that what you expect of your child's future has just changed, in an instant, as soon as you hear the diagnosis. It can mean that you now have a whole bunch of new information to learn and understand in order to help your child. It can also mean that the life you had imagined, as a parent, has also changed. This process of learning and accepting that your child has a disability can be challenging for a parent. However, as discussed in the previous chapter, the advantages for your child in receiving a diagnosis and starting appropriate treatment early are many, and the diagnosis can provide some answers to your concerns.

In this chapter, I provide more specific information on what a diagnosis actually means – along with what it doesn't mean – and some information on how the diagnosis can help you know what to expect for your child and their future.

Receiving a diagnosis

A diagnosis is a label or a name for a specific condition or types of conditions. Some diagnoses refer to a discrete condition; for example, genetic conditions such as Down syndrome, or microdeletions such as 22q11.2 (also known as DiGeorge syndrome). Some diagnoses are an umbrella term for a group of similar presentations, sometimes due to a shared underlying cause; for example cerebral palsy, which refers to a disorder of movement that occurs due to an injury in the developing brain. However, the diagnosis of cerebral palsy covers a multitude of different presentations, with significantly varying levels of ability or difficulties, and significantly varying numbers of associated conditions. Although the symptoms of movement difficulties, abnormalities in muscle tone, and some sort of neurological abnormality are shared by all children with cerebral palsy, each child with cerebral palsy presents differently. Finally, some diagnoses are not particularly definitive at all, and instead are just a descriptive term that describes a child's difficulties. The medical world does not know everything about the body and how it works, or everything about what can cause developmental issues in children. As a result, some children will receive a diagnosis as generic as 'global developmental delay' or older children might be diagnosed with 'intellectual impairment'. These types of diagnoses recognise that the child has an underlying developmental condition, but that we don't yet know why or what is causing it.

Depending on what type of diagnosis your child receives, you may or may not be able to use the diagnosis to better understand what it means for your child and their future abilities. A diagnosis can tell you:

- *The underlying cause of your child's developmental difficulties or disability.* For example, if your child has a diagnosis of cerebral palsy, that tells you their difficulties are due to an interruption or injury (for example, due to infection, inflammation, damage or malformation) that occurred to their infant brain. Or if your child has a genetic diagnosis, such as Down syndrome, a rare genetic syndrome or a microdeletion, that tells you exactly where in their DNA or chromosomes the difference has occurred.

- *For some children, the ideal treatments.* Your child's diagnosis might tell you whether a specific drug can assist with or even mitigate the effects of the condition. For example, if children diagnosed with congenital hypothyroidism take their thyroid replacement hormones, they can be expected to be able to keep up with their peers developmentally.

- *Whether you can expect your child to improve over time or, sadly for some parents and children, whether your child will deteriorate over time.* For example, if a girl is diagnosed with Rett syndrome, we know that her developmental abilities will deteriorate over time.

However, a diagnosis also does not tell you a lot of information. Vast differences can exist between different children who share the same diagnosis. For example, some children with cerebral palsy can walk, talk, run, attend mainstream schooling and have only mild movement difficulties; other children with cerebral palsy require a wheelchair for all of their mobility, have trouble holding their head upright, have limited ability to communicate, and require feeding through a tube. Some children with Down syndrome have mild intellectual difficulties, but can learn and grow up to live independently and work. Other children with Down syndrome have more severe intellectual impairments and will require full-time care their entire life. As a result, your child's diagnosis alone may not be a good indicator of their ultimate future abilities.

For a list of some common diagnoses, and what they mean for your child, see appendix A.

A diagnosis is not a prognosis; a prognosis is not set in stone

An important lesson shared by numerous parents and that I have learnt through experience is that a child's diagnosis is absolutely not their prognosis. A prognosis is the anticipated future function, outcome or life expectancy for a person with a particular condition. I have met children who, based on their diagnosis and early MRIs of their brain, I would not have expected to walk and talk and be the clever children they are. In addition, I have met children who were given a really poor prognosis very early in life, and these children have gone on to be typically developing children with no developmental issues whatsoever. Sometimes the prognosis given is a 'best guess' at the child's future function. Sometimes the prognosis is accurate, and your child might develop closely to the predicted outcome. At other times, however, a child's long-term abilities do not reflect their original presentation or prognosis. This is where neuroplasticity can really make an impact, either through natural recovery or in response to early intervention.

As discussed in chapter 1, neuroplasticity is the ability for the brain to adapt and change, and is high during infancy and early childhood. As a result, if your child has a mild difficulty, this might be permanent or it might be overcome as a result of the brain adapting. And for a small number of children, although this is far less common, even a severe developmental brain insult with a poor prognosis can change markedly due to neuroplasticity. For example, a series of studies performed in the late 1970s and early 1980s by Papile et al. performed CT scans on and tracked developmental outcomes in almost 200 babies born prematurely at a hospital in New Mexico in the United States. The results of this study showed that only 28 per cent of the babies who had a brain bleed went on to have a major disability, including 36 per cent and 76 per cent of babies with a grade 3 or 4 bleed respectively (which indicates a more severe bleed and often means the child would have a more severe difficulties as a result). The remaining infants within the study went on to develop normally. This demonstrates that some infant brains, even following some degree of damage at birth, have the capacity to adapt sufficiently to overcome this damage.

A diagnosis is given to help define the underlying cause for your child's developmental or movement difficulties. But it does not define who your child is and what they can achieve.

Case studies

Mason's mum found out that Mason had severe spina bifida at her 20-week ultrasound scan. Mason was born in a larger tertiary hospital because he needed to have neurosurgery to close his very large spinal lesion a few hours after birth. Based on the size of his lesion, it was anticipated that Mason would have paralysis below the level of his lesion (which was in the middle of his back). But Mason also had some scans of his brain in the first few weeks of his life, which showed marked loss of brain tissue due to hydrocephalus (swelling in the fluid that surrounds the brain). When I received a handover from the physiotherapist looking after him in the NICU, she reported that his MRI showed very limited brain tissue, and that so far Mason had shown very little eye contact and no eye follow, as well as the expected limited movement in the lower half of his body. Based on these early assessments, Mason's prognosis was poor, with concerns he would have limited communication and thinking skills. However, as Mason grew during his first few years of life, he developed really well! As expected, he had complete paralysis below the level of his lesion. However, Mason demonstrated none of the expected difficulties with learning, thinking and communicating. He learnt to move himself around the floor by pulling his body with his hands. He learnt to talk as expected like any other child of his age. And he is now attending mainstream school, and is keeping up with his peers academically.

* * *

Keira was not expected to survive. Keira was (is) a twin, and during her mum's antenatal ultrasound scans, the doctors identified that Keira had extremely severe swelling of the fluid in her brain, or hydrocephalus, which basically prevented her brain tissue from developing. Based on these scans, the medical team felt Keira was highly unlikely to survive for long after birth due to the insufficient brain tissue. Keira's parents prepared to deliver their baby girls, devastatingly expecting that Keira would not survive. Her parents discussed their wishes about how to support Keira when she was born, and what would happen if she deteriorated, and how she would be kept comfortable. Due to the extreme amount of swelling on her brain, her parents decided with the medical team that they would just keep her comfortable, and would not get a shunt inserted to help drain the fluid from her brain (which is normally what would happen if a baby is born with hydrocephalus) because they didn't want to put her through unnecessary trauma if she was not going to survive anyway. When Keira was born, like any baby, she was quickly checked over and then given to her parents to hold so that she could be with her parents and her twin sister. But, unexpectedly, Keira kept breathing steadily. Unexpectedly, she took her first feed. And again unexpectedly, she kept breathing and feeding through to five days. By this point, her parents and medical team had realised that, actually, Keira might survive, and so the decision was made to insert a shunt into her brain to relieve the pressure from the fluid in her brain. I met Keira when she was eight months old (the referral did not come through any earlier for early intervention because it was not expected that Keira would do so well). In the following six months, I saw Keira learn to hold her head up properly, roll to get around the room, sit up independently, and eventually crawl. In addition, she learnt to smile, laugh, explore objects, play and babble. All of these things she was not expected to do. And if you saw the scans of her brain from when she was born, showing hardly any visible brain tissue, you would understand why she was given such a poor prognosis. Yet, she was able to prove everyone's assumptions wrong.

The preceding examples demonstrate how a prognosis for a child may underestimate a child's capabilities. However, not every outcome is so different from the original prognosis. The prognosis for some children with certain diagnoses is much easier to predict, as a result of strong evidence and information about that particular condition, and so their outcomes end up closely reflecting the original prognosis. Sadly, for other children, the original prognosis may have overestimated the future abilities of a child (for example, if the diagnosis was not accurate or if the child experienced complications as a result of their condition such as significant seizures or other medical complications).

So when your child receives a diagnosis, I would suggest taking on board the information you are given about your child's prognosis to help you to prepare and plan ahead for your child, but also being open for the possibilities and opportunities for your child to outdo those original predictions.

Knowing what to expect

Every parent I have ever met whose child has just been diagnosed with a disability usually has a number of questions about the future. Typically these questions include: Will my child walk? Will my child talk? Will they have any other disabilities? Will they go to a mainstream school?

Anticipating your child's future function is important in enabling you to prepare yourself and your child for what the future might hold. Understanding your child's likely or possible future function can help you to think about what your child might need now and in the future, what developmental supports your child might need to help them develop their maximum level of independence, and how to support all areas of their development. This understanding can also help you to know where to focus your energies for therapies, and also start to picture your child's future as it might be, because this will be different to how you might have originally envisaged their life.

However, as discussed in the previous section, at this stage you need to approach this information about your child's possible future function as a general ballpark guide, rather than exactly what you can expect. Again, your child's prognosis is not set in stone, and any description of your child's possible future abilities is purely a best guess. In the following sections, I outline some areas of development for children with various disabilities where we can, with some level of reliability, provide a reasonable estimate of your child's future functioning. However, as well as not knowing specifically how your child will develop, it is also entirely possible that new therapies or interventions will be introduced in the future that improve your child's potential outcomes. It is also entirely possible that your child might experience difficulties that you did not anticipate, such as health issues or seizures that ultimately affect their overall development. So use the information in the following sections as a guide to give you some direction for your child's needs, but also remember that your child might surprise you with their development.

Anticipating the future for children with cerebral palsy

Cerebral palsy is the most common cause of childhood disability. As a result, a lot more research is available on the future abilities and difficulties for children with cerebral palsy than any other diagnosis.

In 2012, an Australian group of paediatric researchers reviewed the research available to determine likely functional abilities and other associated difficulties for children with cerebral palsy. The purpose for this research was to gather information to be able to answer parents' questions about their child's future function and life when their child is first diagnosed with cerebral palsy. This study found that among children with cerebral palsy:

- two in three can walk (this includes children who can walk with walking aids as well as those that can walk independently without any walking aids)
- three in four can speak
- one in two has some form of intellectual disability
- one in three has hip displacement (where the hip migrates out of the hip socket)
- one in four has epilepsy
- one in four has a behavioural disorder
- one in four has bladder control problems
- one in five has a sleep disorder
- one in five dribbles
- one in 10 is blind
- one in 15 requires tube feeding
- one in 25 is deaf.

The study also found that children who have more severe motor impairments and are not able to walk are more likely to experience any of the listed difficulties – except for behavioural difficulties, which could occur equally among all children with cerebral palsy regardless of their level of physical disability.

This study has given health professionals a way to broadly describe to you, the parent, the rates of possible abilities or difficulties for children with cerebral palsy. However, other research is available that can explain more specifically what motor or movement abilities you might expect for your child with cerebral palsy.

Predicting the future gross motor ability for your child with cerebral palsy

In 1997, a group of researchers developed a five-level system that can be used to help classify children with cerebral palsy into meaningfully different levels of motor ability that could be used to predict future motor abilities. This classification system is called the Gross Motor Function Classification System, and it is a very useful tool for identifying a child's current motor function, predicting their likely long-term motor function, and also predicting the likelihood of them experiencing the difficulties or impairments listed.

The following descriptors describe the likely motor ability of a child with cerebral palsy who is aged between 6 and 12 years of age:

- *Level 1:* Children can walk independently without limitations at home, school, outdoors and in the community. They can walk up and down curbs or stairs independently without holding onto a rail. They typically can run and jump, but their speed, balance and coordination are usually decreased.

- *Level 2:* Children walk independently in most settings, but typically experience some limitations such as difficulty walking long distances, and balancing on uneven terrain, inclines, in crowded areas, confined spaces or when carrying objects. Children require the use of a rail or physical assistance to go up and down a curb or stairs, and may require a mobility device for walking long distances. Children at this level have minimal ability in higher level gross motor skills such as running and jumping.

- *Level 3:* Children walk using a hand-held mobility device such as a walking stick, crutches or a walker in most indoor settings. Children require assistance when getting up out of a chair or up off the floor. Children at this level will likely use some form of wheeled mobility for long distances, such as pushing themselves in a wheelchair or using a powered wheelchair.

Receiving a diagnosis and starting early intervention

- *Level 4:* Children primarily mobilise by being pushed in a manual wheelchair or by driving a power wheelchair. At home, children at this level may be able to move about on the floor (roll, creep or crawl), require assistance for transfers, can walk short distances with physical assistance or in a body support walking frame, or use powered mobility devices. Children can stand using a standing frame and can hold their own head up without assistance.

- *Level 5:* Children require a high level of physical support and are pushed in a manual wheelchair in all settings. Children at this level require supportive equipment with high levels of postural supports to keep their body in alignment, including head support to keep their head upright. Children also require full physical assistance for transfers, including the likely need for a hoist when they get bigger. They will be able to use a standing frame that provides adequate trunk and head support.

Using the GMFCS, it is possible for your doctor or therapist to provide you with a reasonable description and expectation of your child's future motor abilities from as early as two years of age. In addition, another assessment (the Hammersmith Infant Neurological Examination or HINE) can be performed by your doctor or therapist from two months to two years of age, which can predict the likelihood of your child having a severe form of cerebral palsy (GMFCS level 4 or 5).

To find out more about the GMFCS, go to https://www.canchild.ca/en/diagnoses/cerebral-palsy and click the Gross Motor Function Classification System link.

Predicting expected rate and plateau of gross motor development for children with cerebral palsy:

In addition to the general descriptions of the GMFCS, research has been able to demonstrate how quickly children of different GMFCS levels will progress, and what ages they start to plateau with their gross motor development. In the following figure (based on information in Rosenbaum, P. et al.; see the 'Further reading' section), you can see that:

- All children with cerebral palsy progress in their gross motor skills early on in childhood, particularly between birth and approximately two to three years of age.
- All children with cerebral palsy plateau with their gross motor skill development. However, the timing of the plateau is related to their GMFCS level, with children with more severe motor impairments plateauing earlier in life than children with milder motor impairments.
- Children with milder motor impairments have a more rapid rate of improvement in their gross motor skills than children with more severe motor impairments.
- Children with more severe cerebral palsy do not develop motor skills to the same level as children with milder cerebral palsy.

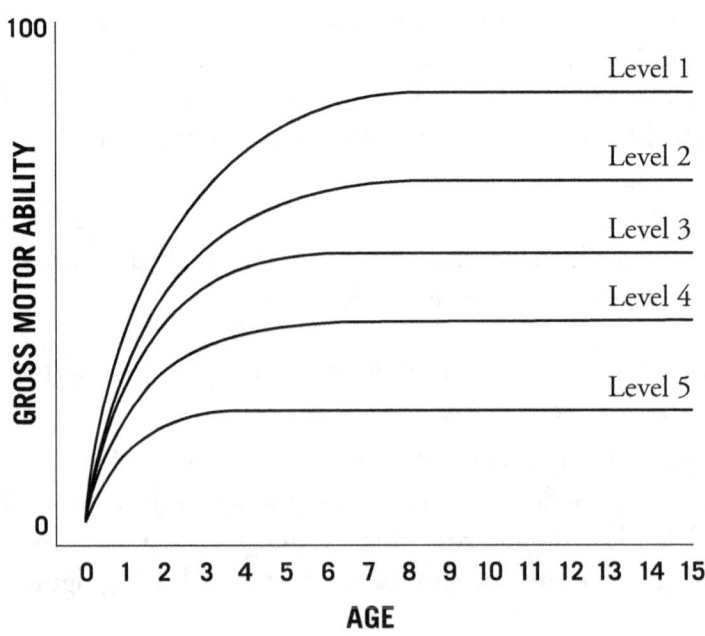

Predicted average development by the Gross Motor Function Classification System levels

Receiving a diagnosis and starting early intervention

What does this mean for your child with cerebral palsy?

- You can expect the most rapid improvements in your child's gross motor skills to occur in their early childhood. This again demonstrates that by receiving early intervention in the first two years of your child's life, you're optimising their opportunities for improvement.

- As your child approaches the age of two, you should be able to more reliably predict their future gross motor function or abilities.

- Your child's achievement of new gross motor skills will plateau at some point during their early childhood, and this will occur earlier for children with more severe motor difficulties.

- Based on your child's GMFCS level, and their anticipated future functional ability, you will be able to start to think about, anticipate and plan for your child's future function.

Again, the best way to comprehend how this works in real life is this is through case studies.

Case studies

Tom was two years old when we started seeing him at our clinic. Tom has cerebral palsy as a result of complications during his mum's pregnancy that resulted in a premature birth. He has quadriplegic cerebral palsy, affecting both his arms and legs, and, at two, was able to hold his head upright, but needed his mum and dad's help around his trunk to sit upright. According to the GMFCS levels, Tom was functioning at a GMFCS Level 4. Based on that, as Tom's therapists, we could anticipate that in the future Tom was likely to require the use of a power wheelchair to be able to independently mobilise around his home and community. Tom was (and is) a motivated and bright boy, and was showing good play and interactive skills within his physical limits. As a result, we discussed and planned with his parents that, as part of Tom's overall therapy plan, we would start trialling some early powered mobility devices so that Tom could learn to move himself independently around his environments in preparation for learning to use a power wheelchair in the future. These devices were introduced, but they did not replace his ongoing therapy to continue to progress his gross motor skills of sitting, standing and some stepping with assistance. By introducing powered mobility skills early, Tom was able to master these skills in his early childhood so that he was very proficient in using his power wheelchair when he started school a few years later.

*　*　*

Sally was born slightly early because she was a twin, but had no remarkable concerns at the time of her birth. Sally walked slightly later than her twin, but still learned to walk at around 18 months. However, Sally tended to always walk up on her toes on her right leg. Sally was referred to us at our clinic at two years of age. At this stage, Sally was continuing to walk up on the toes of her right leg. After her assessment, which identified signs that Sally might have underlying cerebral palsy, I was able to confidently discuss with her mum that Sally would walk independently, but that she might have difficulties with running, jumping, hopping, skipping and other higher level motor skills. As a result, we chose to focus her therapy on improving her walking pattern, and then improving Sally's higher level motor skills.

Anticipating motor function for children with Down syndrome

It is well known that children with Down syndrome achieve their motor and developmental skills later than typically developing children. This is due to a combination of physical differences and, at varying levels, cognitive differences.

The differences that affect the development of children with Down syndrome include:

- *Joint hypermobility:* Children with Down syndrome have extra flexible joints, which means their muscles have to work harder to keep their joints stable when they are developing skills that bring them upright against gravity such as sitting, standing and walking.

- *Low muscle tone:* This describes the child's resting level of muscle activity. Children with Down syndrome have 'floppier' and less 'tense' muscles at rest. This means they have to contract their muscles harder to get the same strength as a child without low muscle tone, and that they have to develop higher levels of strength to move their bodies and to develop motor skills.

- *Shortened limbs:* The long bones in the arms and legs of children with Down syndrome are shorter than typically developing children, which changes slightly the way their body is able to move.

- *Cognitive differences:* These can be very variable in children with Down syndrome. Some children can have relatively typical cognitive levels, and others can have significant intellectual impairment. Cognitive difficulties can affect a child's ability to learn to move and learn new skills, because they have less ability, interest and motivation to explore their environment and make sense of the things in it.

The table included in appendix B provides a general guide for when children with Down syndrome might be expected to achieve certain developmental milestones. However, due to the variations between different children with Down syndrome, the achievement of these milestones is highly varied, so your child might achieve these motor milestones earlier or later than is listed in the table. It is also important to know that while children with Down syndrome require more time to learn movements or skills, especially as the difficulty of the movement increases, the severity of their impairments affect the rate of their skill development, but not their ultimate or upper limit of abilities.

To illustrate how a diagnosis of Down syndrome with a prognosis of developmental delay may not actually affect developmental progress, I can compare one girl we were seeing at our clinic with my own children. When I had my son (my second child), we were seeing a little girl with Down syndrome at our clinic who was developing really, really well. This little girl crawled at eight months, stood at 10 to 11 months, and took her first independent steps shortly after at 12 months. In the meantime, my 'typically developing' children had both crawled at about 11 months, pulled to stand between 12 and 14 months, and walked at 16 to 18 months of age – much later than our little client!

Anticipating functional abilities for children with autism

As a general rule, it is expected that all children with autism will learn to walk. In addition, many will learn to run, jump, climb and swing, but they may take longer to achieve motor milestones and will often have difficulties in performing these to a high level, due to difficulties with motor control, motor planning, balance and coordination.

In regards to their other areas of function, a difficulty shared by all children with autism is social and communication skills, although significant variation exists in these difficulties between children. Every child with autism is different, so it is harder to anticipate how much your child might progress over time. One study by Poon, K. et al. (see the 'Further reading' section) showed that young children (between 9 and 18 months of age) with autism who demonstrated higher levels of shared attention (following another's eye gaze or point, and directing another's attention), imitation (imitating actions on or with objects), and object play (playing or interacting with an object, such as a toy) had higher communication and IQ scores between three and seven years of age.

Anticipating future function for children with other conditions

Depending on what your child's underlying diagnosis is, it may or may not be possible to predict what their future skills will be. If your child has a common genetic condition, you might be able to find resources and information that describes how children with that condition commonly develop. If your child has a rare genetic condition, that kind of information might not be readily available, or the information available might be quite vague. Instead, you might be able to find out some information by making contact with other parents around the world whose child also has that condition. Alternatively, if your child's condition is not yet diagnosed, your best attempt at anticipating your child's future function could be discussing this with your child's medical and therapy team – unfortunately, however, we sometimes cannot give you any more information than what you already have about what the future might hold for your child.

Anticipating other functional abilities such as communication, fine motor, or cognitive function

The ability to predict your child's hand function, communication ability, and social or interactive skills is a harder thing to do. Less research is available on these various skills, and the improvements in relation to age are less predictable. In terms of cerebral palsy, in my experience I have seen children with severe forms of cerebral palsy learn to speak using an electronic device in their late childhood or early teenage years. I have also seen teenage boys finally master hand skills like tying their own shoelaces. The following outlines some generalised predictions based on my knowledge and experience of working with many children with cerebral palsy:

- Children with dystonic cerebral palsy often have difficulty communicating using their own voice, but many can learn to communicate very well using augmentative alternative communication devices such as communication boards, books or electronic programs.

- Generally speaking, the lower your child's GMFCS level (that is, Levels 1 to 2), the more likely that they will be able to communicate by talking and writing like their typically developing peers (unless they have dystonic or dyskinetic cerebral palsy, or a significant intellectual impairment).

- Children with hemiplegic cerebral palsy generally have better hand function than children with quadriplegic cerebral palsy. This is because they have at least one hand that functions well. Many of the tasks that we use our hands for in daily life we can manage using only one hand and an assisting arm. Children with hemiplegic cerebral palsy, even if their affected hand is really limited in what it can do, can often learn new ways to effectively use their good hand for functional tasks and their wrist/forearm/elbow/chin/other body part to act as a stabiliser.

- A child's ability to play (and by this I mean engage with toys and others in a variety of different ways) can sometimes be a good indicator of a child's future communication and cognitive ability.

CHAPTER FOUR

Considering your approach to helping your child

As the previous chapters have already outlined, early intervention can provide the best outcomes for your child. But before you dive into helping your child, it is important to also become aware of the emotional aspects of considering your child's future and getting started with treatment. While the treatment journey might seem reasonably straightforward – your child needs help with their development, so your job is to go out and find help and get started – it has the potential to be filled with a roller-coaster of emotions that could affect your confidence. You continuing to feel confident that you are doing what you can for your child is vital, and this is why it is important to consider, ahead of time, the impact of your approach and how the process of helping your child might play out.

Being aware of the emotional roller-coaster

The process of recognising that your child might have some developmental concerns, seeking help and possible answers, receiving a diagnosis, learning about what that might mean for your child, and then getting started on treatment can often be experienced by parents as a roller-coaster of emotions. These emotions come from:

- recognising or identifying developmental issues (perhaps making you concerned, worried, anxious, fearful)
- seeking help to get answers (causing worry, frustration at delays in seeing someone or, if getting answers quickly, overwhelm with the diagnostic process)
- receiving a diagnosis (which can come with grief, disbelief and denial, relief to finally have some answers, worry and fear for the future)
- learning about what that might mean for your child (again causing grief, worry, confidence that you have a better understanding of what to expect, or frustration at the lack of information).

Even before you get started on treatment to help your child, you have likely experienced some or many of the emotions listed, meaning this can be a pretty draining time for parents. Before you dive into getting started on treatment, it might be useful to give yourself some time to process the information you have received and how you feel about it all, and to regroup as a parent and family who now have additional things to consider within your day-to-day life as well as your future.

The process of commencing your child's treatment can also bring with it a variety of emotions that have the potential to disrupt your confidence as a parent who is trying to do the best they can for their child. Initially you may feel positive that you finally have some information and that you are getting started on treatment. You may feel empowered that you are finally doing something to help your child. You may also experience joy and feel really optimistic that, with some

Considering your approach to helping your child

extra supports, your child is starting to show some exciting improvements or progress. However, on the flip side, it is also common for some parents to feel anxious about making sure they are doing everything they can for their child, overwhelmed at the time commitment you now need to give to things like therapy appointments, home programs and meetings with funding agencies, or frustrated that you have to wait to access treatment or that your child is not showing the improvements or progress that you had hoped to see.

The process of starting treatment can also be challenging for your child. Some children will enjoy the extra attention and will show progress from early on, while other children can become overwhelmed, can be fearful of new therapy providers, or feel frustrated at themselves or with others. You can also expect that, as your child starts to be challenged, their behaviour and self-regulation might also be affected – because it genuinely is really hard for them and they can feel fearful, frustrated, anxious or even just fatigued.

As you start this roller-coaster, keep in mind three important things:

- Helping your child through early intervention should be viewed as a long-term process, rather than a quick fix. While you might experience early wins from starting intervention, many children require ongoing care and support for many years, and it is possible that therapy providers, support services and health professionals will be involved in your child throughout their life (to varying degrees). Try not to put pressure on yourself or your child if you are not seeing gains immediately. Even if you are not seeing gains, you and your child are laying down a foundation of trust, rapport and basic functional skills that will put them in the best position to achieve the best they can in the future.

- Continue to ask questions if you are feeling confused or are not sure about something. The process of receiving a diagnosis can be a bit of a whirlwind, and you can be given a lot of information in a short period of time. Continue discussing your concerns and asking questions to build your confidence in being able to understand and manage your child's needs, and being able to make decisions about your child's care, rather than just being told something and accepting it.

- If you are feeling unsure, uncertain, uneasy or uncomfortable about an aspect of your child's treatment, it is important that you feel empowered to switch your child's treatment or management plans, in consultation with an expert you trust.

Taking your time …

As much as you might want to race into helping your child and helping them improve, some things are worth taking your time over:

- Take your time learning about and understanding your child's condition and needs. Ask questions, look up information, and take time to digest it all.

- Take your time learning to understand your child's future. Give yourself time to grieve the life you had previously imagined for your child, and start to imagine and dream about what a good life for your child could look like now.

- Take your time to find the therapists and services that suit your child and family. Try to find therapists and service providers that are a good match to your child and family. Consider your child's and family's needs, your values and approach to life.

- Allow your child's therapists time to get to know your child. Understanding a child – their personality, quirks, interests, strengths, abilities and challenges – can take time. If your child's therapist can develop a deep understanding of your child – in both the initial assessment and over time – the therapist will more confidently be able to pinpoint the best way to help your child, with greater clarity and certainty.

- Similarly, allow your child time to get to know their therapists and support providers. Therapy is a collaborative process, with the therapist and the child working together. Therapy should never be done *to* your child; it should always be done *with* your child. Your child will more willingly and happily be an active participant in therapy if they have had time to get to know the therapist and have built their own level of trust and confidence in them.

- Give your child time to learn and master a new skill before pushing for them to move onto the next skill. Mastery of a skill takes a lot of practice. Hundreds and thousands of repetitions. Even though it might feel like your child is not progressing because they are continuing to practise the same skill, achieving this mastery is actually preparing them to learn the next, more complex, movement or skill. Your child will develop new skills by layering them on top of skills they have already mastered. So the time your child spends repetitively mastering a skill is time well spent.

Focusing on *how* rather than *when*

As already touched on, moving using poor or suboptimal movement patterns can lead to more difficulty when trying to develop higher level skills and can also cause longer term complications. Because of this, *how* a child learns to do something – walking, for example – can be more important than *when* they do it.

Let's look at idiopathic toe walking as an example. Idiopathic toe walking is a condition in which children with no underlying medical or developmental condition consistently and persistently walk on their toes. Children with idiopathic toe walking are typically developing children – they almost always learn to walk within the normal times frames expected for children to walk independently (9 to 18 months). However, *how* they walk is not optimal, and the quality of their walk is not optimal, and this can lead to problems such as muscle contractures, or joint deformities later down the track if these movement problems are not addressed early.

Postural differences between children who toe walk and children who don't

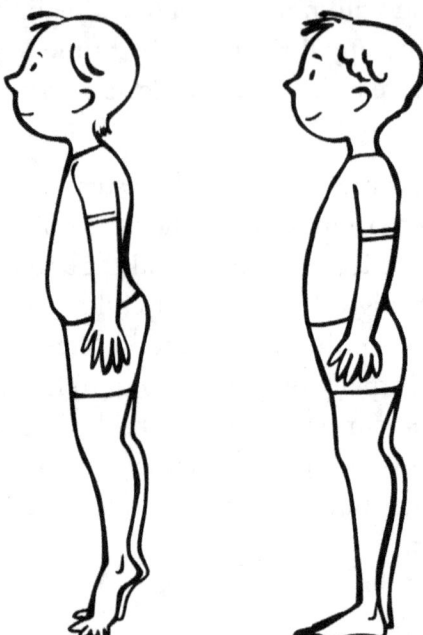

Case studies

Chloe and Jacob are two little people we see in our clinic who both have mild cerebral palsy. Both have one side of their body affected (hemiplegia), with both their arm and their leg affected. Both can walk, both can talk. Chloe can use her affected hand a little better than Jacob can. When assessing their spasticity (a neurological sign that impacts how a muscle activates and how flexible it is when moving it), Jacob definitely has more spasticity present than Chloe, and you can see that in how he uses his hand. However, when it comes to their walking, surprisingly, Jacob walks with a better pattern than Chloe. How is it that Jacob, who neurologically has slightly worse signs and symptoms, can walk with a better pattern than Chloe? This is due to the fact that Chloe was diagnosed at the age of five – much later than Jacob, who was diagnosed at eight months of age.

Chloe learnt to walk at approximately 18 months of age, same as Jacob. But because no-one had identified that Chloe had cerebral palsy, she didn't receive any early intervention. For the first four years that Chloe walked, she walked up on her toes, with her knees slightly bent, especially on her right side. At the age of six, even after 18 months of therapy, Chloe still found it very difficult to keep her right knee straight when she was standing on it when walking – even with a splint (an ankle foot orthosis (AFO)) on her right ankle. In comparison, Jacob received early intervention *prior* to him learning to walk. This meant that his therapist could anticipate the difficulties he might experience with walking, and the movement patterns he might then adopt, and take steps to prevent them. Unlike Chloe, Jacob started wearing an AFO splint just as he was starting to learn to stand and take steps, which helped him to keep his knee straight and land on his heel when he was walking. As a result, Jacob learnt to walk using a typical heel-toe pattern, providing a foundation for him to learn more challenging upright skills such as running, going up stairs, jumping and hopping, and helping to prevent him from developing complications such as muscle tightening and leg length differences as he grows.

Another example is children with Down syndrome learning to walk – and, again, quality of movement should take priority over achievement of independent walking within expected time frames. The typical age for a child with Down syndrome to learn to walk independently is approximately two years of age. But just like typically developing children, this 'typical' age is very variable. In our clinic, we have had children with Down syndrome learn to walk at 12 months (as already mentioned, before both of my children!), and we have had children with Down syndrome learn to walk at three years of age. At our clinic, we are not worried about the age at which these children learn to walk – again, we are more concerned with *how* they walk. Our treatments are directed towards ensuring these children have great movement patterns that provide a foundation for them to be able to learn to stand and walk with optimal alignment, posture and muscle activation, so that they continue to develop movement patterns that will provide a foundation for the movement skills they will need to learn in the future.

But what if your child is not going to learn to walk anytime near the expected age? We will address this in detail in part III, where I look at developing independence. However, one aspect is important to note here. Some children with physical disabilities will not ever learn to walk. Some children with physical disabilities will learn to walk much, much later than expected (we have had some children learn to walk independently at seven or eight years of age). So what is more important for these children – the timing or how they learn to walk? Well, the answer to this is actually a bit of both. If we know a child is not going to learn to walk, or is not going to learn to move their body so they can independently get themselves around their environment from A to B, we will work with the child and the family to figure out an alternative way to move independently. This might be with a wheelchair, a power wheelchair, or using a walking frame. But, at the same time, when we are working towards them learning to stand and walk, we will also be making sure that *how* they are learning to stand and walk is as good as we can get it.

Dealing with developmental progressions and plateaus

The final little bit of the puzzle in understanding the roller-coaster of child development is that *all* children will go through developmental progressions and then developmental plateaus. As a child is learning new skills, they will be progressing. Each day you might see them doing something new that they couldn't do the previous day or week. They might be learning to roll, learning to reach and grasp, learning to bring a toy to their mouth, and learning to make cooing sounds. So many new things. But then in a week or two, you might notice that your child's developmental progress seems to have stopped. Perhaps they haven't done anything new in a few weeks. Sometimes they might not have done anything new in a few months. This can be a worrying and anxious time for a parent of a child with a disability. But – assuming your child's fundamental needs are being met (such as food, shelter, safety and belonging), and that they are continuing to receive opportunities to practise their developmental skills – these periods of time without progress, which I call 'developmental plateaus', are not cause for concern and are equally as important to your child's development as the periods of progress are. During these plateaus, your child is refining and mastering all the previous skills they have already learnt. This provides them with a solid foundation of skills from which to, in time, learn the next skills in the developmental process. Instead of noticing that your child is or isn't learning new skills, look for how your child is improving, refining or mastering their current skills. Ask yourself:

- Is my child steadier when they do that movement?
- Do they have more control when they do that activity?
- Are they more accurate when they are reaching/grasping/letting go/speaking?
- Are they able to do that movement or activity more quickly?
- Can they do that action or skill more smoothly, and with less effort?

For example, your child might have learnt to sit many months ago, and perhaps has not yet learnt to move from sitting to crawling on their tummy. However, more subtle improvements might include:

- Your child can now sit with their legs closer together than they previously could.
- They can now reach much further to get their toys.
- They now look so much straighter in their back when sitting than previously.

- They can now hold toys in their hands and can lift them up high without toppling over like they used to.

Each of these examples shows an improvement in *how* your child is performing a learnt task, rather than the achievement of a whole new task. And each of these examples demonstrates that your child is mastering their sitting skills in preparation for learning the next skill in their developmental progress, which is usually moving on the floor by creeping or crawling.

Keeping the end in mind

When starting out with getting help for your child, and throughout your child's treatment journey, it is important to always keep the end goal in mind. In the end, what do you want for your child? What is the purpose of doing all the therapies and treatments? For each family, this end goal or vision might be slightly different. However, it is important for every parent of a child with a disability to remember that the purpose of any therapy or treatment for your child should be for them to develop as much independence as possible. And the more independence they develop, and the more capable they are – eventually, your child might not need treatment or therapies anymore or as frequently. This is what I describe as the therapy journey – while your child might start out receiving lots of therapy and treatment when they are little – the amount and frequency of therapy should ideally decrease over time. And the reason for the decrease is because your child should eventually be able to participate in activities in the community with their friends and peers, which they will do instead of the 1:1 therapy that they started out with. So if your child's therapist recommends that your child doesn't need to be seen as often, or no longer needs therapy (instead they might just need regular reviews), try not to feel anxious about this and instead see this for the success that it actually is.

CHAPTER FIVE

Being aware of future difficulties and changes

The process of being aware of and acting on concerns as early as possible does not end after your child has received a diagnosis. Like any child, your child's needs will change over time. With growth and development can come changes – some of which may be improvements, while others may be problems or signal deterioration. Like with those early developmental changes you first noticed in your child, being aware of and acting early on any problems or changes give your child the best chance of fixing those changes, or minimising their impact as much as is possible.

Anticipating future difficulties

As well as anticipating your child's likely future functional abilities, as discussed in chapter 3, your doctors or therapists may also consider and anticipate possible future difficulties, and help you to prevent or address these early to optimise your child's outcomes. Possible future difficulties might include joint contractures (stiffening of the joints), muscle shortening, scoliosis, maladaptive movement patterns, loss of function as your child gets older and heavier, or inability to keep up in the classroom when writing with a pencil. By identifying what problems your child is at risk of, and taking steps to either minimise them or prevent them, your child has the best chance to continue to develop their individual full capacity.

The following sections provide three key examples of possible difficulties and how they relate to ongoing early intervention for children with disabilities.

Children with hemiplegic cerebral palsy not using their affected hand and arm

Children with hemiplegic cerebral palsy have one side of their body affected; for example, a child with cerebral palsy affecting his right side will have difficulties with the movements of his right arm, right leg, and the right side of his trunk. We know that almost all children with hemiplegic cerebral palsy tend to fall into the GMFCS levels of 1 or 2 (refer to chapter 3), so they will learn to walk independently and walking will be the main way they get around. However, not all children with hemiplegic cerebral palsy learn to use their affected hand and arm very well.

When children are learning to move on the ground – learning to roll, learning to creep forward and around in circles on their belly, and crawling on their hands and knees – they need to use their upper body – their arms and hands – as well as their trunk and legs to manoeuvre and move themselves around. They have to use their arms and legs as props, and they have to control their trunk position to move. In contrast, once children have learnt to walk – although they are constantly and repeatedly practising using their affected leg and foot – they no longer have to use their affected arm and hand anywhere near as much as they did when they were on the floor; the arm can just hang by their side.

As a result, when I treat children with hemiplegic cerebral palsy, I initially focus more on their ability to move on the floor,

Being aware of future difficulties and changes

and their use of their arm, so that their affected hand can become a useful helping or assisting hand for their dominant unaffected hand. Although I do help them learn to get up to standing and to walk, I don't push standing and walking in those early stages because I confidently know that they are going to be able to do this eventually. (Note that this approach is very different for children with cerebral palsy that affects both sides of their body, which I will explain in the following section.)

I saw an example of not following this approach as a young physio, when I travelled through Malaysian Borneo on holiday. As part of a tour, our group took a bus and a boat to stay in a very remote 'long house' (a communal house that is a bit like a set of small house units side by side with a large communal verandah). The bus trip was approximately three hours, along dirt roads, and then we had to get in a long boat and travel down a river for approximately an hour. The long house was located on the river edge, and from what I could tell, was only accessible by boat. While we were staying at the long house, I met a young man, aged approximately 18, who was one of the sons of the elders of the long house. He had hemiplegic cerebral palsy. He was able to walk and to talk, but he had pretty limited hand function and he had a severe contracture of his ankle on his affected side. Based on the geography and the lengths it took our group to get there, I am pretty sure this boy's access to early intervention would have been very, very limited, even non-existent. However, he was able to walk – a great example demonstrating how children with hemiplegic cerebral palsy are likely to be able to walk, regardless of their level of early intervention. However, him not being able to use his affected hand was also potentially indicative of the fact that once he got up to walk, he was not forced to use his hand, and so he was able to develop ways to get by using primarily one hand.

Children with diplegic or quadriplegic cerebral palsy not moving differently on either side of their body

Children with diplegic or quadriplegic cerebral palsy have difficulty moving one side differently to how the other side is moving. When a child with diplegic or quadriplegic cerebral palsy tries to straighten one leg, for example, they often straighten the other as well (without meaning to). In addition, we also know that children with diplegic or quadriplegic cerebral palsy are at risk of developing joint and muscle contractures (stiffness and rigidity) in their leg joints and muscles. As a result, when I am treating children with cerebral palsy affecting both sides of their body, I might not teach them to crawl on their hands and knees. Instead, I might aim to firstly teach them to move their body by moving one side separately to the other – for example, I might help them to learn to move one leg while the other one is held straight. Secondly, I might aim to get the child up into a standing position as soon as possible, so that the muscles and joints in their legs can be stretched and strengthened.

Specifically teaching a child with diplegic or quadriplegic cerebral palsy to stand and walk may be more beneficial than teaching them to crawl, because it will help them to avoid developing joint contractures in their legs. (In contrast, most therapists will intentionally and specifically teach a child with hemiplegic cerebral palsy to crawl, because we know they are going to walk.) What can happen when you teach a child with diplegic or quadriplegic cerebral palsy to crawl, is that they instead learn how to 'bunny hop' – this is where they pull both legs forwards at the same time underneath their body when they are on their hands and knees, and then they reach forwards with both arms together, then pull both knees under them, repeating this over and over to move themselves forwards on the floor. So instead of working on crawling with children with diplegic or quadriplegic cerebral palsy, I am more likely to treat them in a standing position, if possible without them holding onto anything with their hands. When I bring them up into a standing position, in order to move, the child needs to learn to step. When you step, one leg is straight and still, and one leg is bending and moving, so the legs are dissociating from each other. Learning to dissociate one leg from another in standing can carry over to the position of hands and knees – meaning some children will learn to crawl with one leg at a time using a normal reciprocal pattern *after* they have learnt to dissociate their legs from each other in a standing position.

Case study

Ben was a little guy with diplegic cerebral palsy who was referred to see us when he was approximately 18 months old. His mum's goal was for Ben to learn to crawl and sit up by himself. His previous therapists had been working on crawling, but Ben hadn't yet shown any ability to crawl by himself. During my assessment I helped Ben to stand, and he was able to stand quite well, but he couldn't yet dissociate his legs from each other. I had a discussion with Mum, and explained that I wanted to get Ben into a standing position to teach him to move his legs separately, which might then help him to learn to crawl anyway because he would be able to move his legs separately. So for the next three to four weeks, we saw Ben once a week for an hour, and we worked on his ability to move his weight over to one leg and to step with the other leg. Ben picked this up really well, and was showing a really good emerging ability to dissociate his legs. After about four sessions of this, at our next session, Ben's mum told us that he had learnt to crawl on his hands and knees! Ben had learnt to crawl without us even working on crawling!

Children with Down syndrome or low muscle tone not standing in good alignment

Children with Down syndrome and children with some genetic conditions often have hypermobility of their joints and low muscle tone. This means that when they start to bring their body upright against gravity, they find it difficult to generate enough strength in their muscles to keep their joints and their body in good alignment. As a result, when children with these conditions first learn to stand and step, they almost always do so with very flat feet, their knees locked straight, and their legs really wide. This position allows them to be stable, but it is not a very efficient position for stepping and walking. As a therapist, I know that children move most efficiently if they are in a good position to start the movement. As a result, I will frequently recommend children with Down syndrome get orthotics for their feet and ankles at around the time they start pulling to stand – this helps them to bring their feet in underneath their body, and stand with proper alignment of their feet, ankles, knees and hips, which makes learning to stand and learning to step a much easier and much more efficient movement.

Teaching children who have difficulties with hand skills to use an iPad or computer early

If a child is demonstrating difficulties with their hand skills, particularly hand skills around writing and using a pencil, as they are approaching school age (so around four or five), the child's therapist might start to teach them how to use an iPad or a computer keyboard. Although this might seem early for little kids to be using technology, the therapist is anticipating that while the child might cope with using a pencil for the first year or maybe two of school, once the expectation for their handwriting output increases, the child is likely to have difficulty keeping up in the classroom. As a result, the therapist is anticipating this difficulty, and teaching the child an alternative strategy to ensure they can continue to keep up with their school work, ensuring their opportunity for learning is not disadvantaged by their physical skills.

The impact of growth on your child's body

Whenever children grow, their bones grow first, and then their muscles catch up. For typically developing children, they lose flexibility in their muscles for a short period of time, and then their muscles lengthen to match the new length of their bones. However, for children with physical disability who already have tight muscles, the growth of the bones can further tighten the already tight muscles.

Being aware of future difficulties and changes

This continual increased tightening of the muscles as the child grows can cause contracture of the muscles and joints, which can then cause deterioration in their physical abilities. In addition, the tight muscles can also cause the bones to grow less. For children with hemiplegic cerebral palsy, the bones on the affected side of their body might not grow as long or big as the bones on the unaffected side, causing a difference in the length of their arms and legs. By being aware of these potential changes, and taking steps to either prevent or treat any growth changes as early as possible, you and your child's key health professionals can help to prevent any deterioration in your child's abilities, as well as prevent them from experiencing pain.

Another example is the impact of growth on the spine and the potential for the development of scoliosis for children with any form of physical disability. A child might be at risk of developing a scoliosis for many reasons – they might not have very good strength of their trunk muscles, or they might sit or move asymmetrically, or they might have a skeletal abnormality that impacts on their bony growth. Regardless of the cause, during a growth spurt, all children with even the smallest amount of scoliosis are at risk of that scoliosis getting worse. By being aware of this risk, your child's treating therapy team can put into place strategies to try to prevent the scoliosis occurring or prevent any deterioration.

Being aware throughout childhood

I believe that the concept and application of early identification and intervention should also continue beyond infancy and the time of first identification and possible diagnosis. Along with looking out for known future difficulties (as already covered in this chapter), early identification and intervention also includes identifying any secondary issues that might arise as a result of your child's condition or disability, and aiming to prevent or treat those issues and problems as early as possible to mitigate the impact they might have on your child.

Children with physical disabilities change as they grow, which can bring about new or changed difficulties that should be addressed as early as possible to prevent complications or functional deterioration. An example of this is hip surveillance programs for children with cerebral palsy or similar conditions. We know that children with cerebral palsy, or children with neurodevelopmental conditions that cause tight muscles and affect their ability to walk are at risk of their hip migrating out of their socket, resulting in loss of movement at the hips, loss of mobility and function, and pain. Hip surveillance programs screen children for hip dysplasia, migration or dislocation from the time that they are diagnosed through until the child is old enough for the risk to be minimised, and so aim to minimise its occurrence.

So it is important for you and your child's healthcare team to regularly check in and review your child, to screen for and/or identify any issues as early as possible. If you notice something is not quite right with your child no matter their age or where they are in their treatment, I encourage you to seek help from your child's team of health professionals, or alternatively from a new health professional. You, more than anyone, will get to know and understand your child from the inside-out – their needs, their likes and dislikes, and how they tell you if they are happy, scared or in pain. As a result, you are in the best position to be able to monitor and notice if something has changed. If you do identify something has changed or notice a new problem, please follow the same process explained in earlier chapters – seek help early, know how to make sure you are heard, and trust your gut and seek a second opinion if you are not happy with the first.

You are a powerful voice for your child, so I urge you to make sure you remain aware throughout their childhood for any problems or issues. By identifying and treating these as early as possible, you can help to prevent or minimise them impacting on your child's life as much as possible.

Being aware (and acting early) summary points

- The sooner you can identify and get help for your child's needs, the sooner your child can improve.

- You know your child better than anyone else. If you are concerned about your child's development, trust your gut and seek help early.

- No 'bad outcomes' come from seeking an opinion or getting help for your child early.

- A diagnosis is not a prognosis. A prognosis is not set in stone. A diagnosis does not define who your child is and what they can achieve.

- Take your time when starting early intervention. Learn about your child's needs, what you might expect for their future, and find therapists and services that suit your child and family.

- Focus on the quality of your child's skills, not just how quickly they are progressing, to ensure continued progress and to prevent longer term complications.

- Progressions and plateaus are to be expected. During plateaus, your child is refining and mastering all the previous skills they have already learnt, providing them with a solid foundation from which to, in time, learn the next skills.

- Be aware of what your child's future might look like. This can help you to prepare your child to be as independent as possible when they are older.

- Continue to be aware throughout childhood of any possible changes or difficulties your child might encounter as they grow and get older, and seek help for them early.

Part II: Recognise your child's needs

As you learn about and become more aware of your child's needs, you may find yourself with a list of current or potential issues. However, how do you know where to start? How do you know where to focus your efforts, and how do you know what is important and what is not? For many parents, discovering their child's needs can be an overwhelming process.

At our clinic we see quite a few children with multiple developmental issues. One of these children is Phoebe. Phoebe is two years old and has an as yet undiagnosed condition affecting all areas of her development. Phoebe has difficulties in the following areas:

- She is able to crawl short distances and sit for short periods, but is not yet able to sit for long periods of time, to stand, to step or walk.

- She is able to use her hands to grasp and release toys, and she can shake and scratch at toys, but she does not yet know how to manipulate toys, and her play skills are limited to shaking, scratching and mouthing toys.

- She is not yet able to communicate. Phoebe does not have any words, and has limited use of gestures to communicate her wants and needs.

- She is not showing any indication or awareness of when she poos or wees, she is not assisting with dressing herself, and she is just starting to finger feed herself. Most of the time her parents need to spoon feed her.
- Phoebe has a visual impairment, and wears glasses to help her see, but she also likely has a difficulty interpreting the information her eyes see (a cortical visual impairment).

As you can see, Phoebe has multiple delays and multiple issues that need to be addressed. As a parent, this can be overwhelming, and I know it certainly has been for Phoebe's mum. With so many issues that need addressing, where should she start with therapy?

The thing is – all areas of your child's development are interconnected. Working on one area will always have an impact on another area. And missing or not focusing on one area will always affect another area. And, frequently, you may end up working on multiple areas at the same time, because they are so interconnected.

The chapters in this part aim to help you to make sense of all of your child's areas of development, and how they affect each other. I take you through how children typically develop – physically and also in the context of all of the variables that might impact on their development – how to identify your child's strengths, as well as their areas of need, and set goals or focus areas for their development. Finally, I run through the steps you can take to get the help you need, through choosing service providers and treatment programs that match your child and family.

CHAPTER SIX

The interconnectedness of child development

In order to recognise your child's developmental needs and potential, and to take steps to start helping them to achieve progress, you first need to understand some fundamentals about how children develop and, most importantly, how these aspects are connected. This chapter walks you through all the different areas of a child's development, and how they relate to each other.

Different aspects of child development

The first step to recognising your child's needs is to understand the breadth of the different areas of child development. The following sections run through the different areas that affect or are part of your child's development.

Health and wellbeing

Underlying every child's development is their health and wellbeing. Your child's health and wellbeing includes things like the ability to breathe, and having a regular heartbeat, an appropriate body temperature, adequate nutrition, shelter from the elements and mental wellbeing. Your child's health and wellbeing is fundamental to their development. I explain this in more detail later in this chapter, but it is worthwhile mentioning here the body systems that are involved or may have an impact on your child's development:

- *Cardiovascular system:* This includes the heart, lungs, arteries and veins, and is used to circulate the blood around the body to deliver oxygen and remove waste.

- *Gastrointestinal system:* Including the oesophagus, stomach, intestines and rectum, this system absorbs nutrients for the body, and eliminates waste.

- *Neurological system:* Including the brain, nerves and sensory system, this collects and processes information coming in from the body (such as pain, or seeing or hearing something), and sends messages to the body to allow movement or an action.

- *Musculoskeletal system:* Including muscles and joints, this system holds and moves the body.

- *Integumentary system:* This includes skin, hair, nails, sweat glands, and sensory nerves in the skin, and is used to protect the body, to help maintain body temperature, and feel.

- *Endocrine system:* This controls the body's hormones, which are used to influence many functions in the body including growth, metabolism and energy levels.

- *Immune system:* This covers the body's ability to defend itself against illnesses or infections.

- *Renal and urinary system:* Including the kidneys, bladder and urinary tract, this system clears waste and toxins from the blood.

The interconnectedness of child development

Gross motor development

Gross motor development describes all the large motor activities a child typically learns. These activities include holding their head upright, rolling, sitting up, moving on the floor (creeping on their belly or crawling), pulling up to standing, standing, and stepping and walking. It also includes what we call 'higher level' gross motor skills, such as standing on one leg, jumping, hopping, balancing, and throwing, catching and kicking a ball.

Fine motor development (hand and manipulative skills)

Fine motor development describes the smaller motor activities a child typically learns. These activities include pointing, reaching for, holding and letting go of an object, holding 'tools' such as pens and pencils, hammers, cutlery, pegs and cups, and manipulating objects. Fine motor development also includes the ability to use both hands together. This area of development is very important for your child's self-care – fine motor skills allow your child to do up their buttons, zippers and laces, for example, and to clean their teeth, brush and do their hair, feed themselves and prepare meals. Fine motor development is also important for your child's learning, through the use of handwriting or computers and other technology.

Oromotor development

Oromotor development refers to the development of the movements of the mouth, lips, tongue and throat. This area includes the development of sucking and swallowing, and coordinating that with breathing, along with the development of the ability to chew solids adequately, move the food around the mouth, and swallow safely. It also includes the ability to position the mouth, lips, tongue and throat to be able to make sounds for talking and communicating.

Speech and language development

Speech and language development refers to the ability to understand and comprehend language, as well as communicate to others.

It includes spoken language and written language, aided language using signing or communication devices, as well as 'unspoken' language such as gestures, social cues, facial expressions and visual contact.

Cognitive development

Cognitive development refers to your child's thinking, exploration and problem-solving skills. It includes their ability to learn new things and recall that information, comprehend and interpret what they see and hear, build links between different things they have learnt, adapt their learnings to different situations, and plan. It is important to know that children with even very significant physical disability who cannot speak can have good cognitive development.

Social and emotional development

Social development refers to your child's ability to interact and engage with other people in their world. It also refers to your child's ability to understand and control their own feelings and behaviours, as well as understand the feelings of other people.

Environment

The environment in which your child lives and attends day care or school, and your neighbourhood and community, all have a role to play in your child's development. When referring to the environment, included is the physical environment and spaces, the cultural environment, and the people within the environment.

Your child's personality

Every child is born with a unique, in-built personality. Your child's personality can be seen from very early on in life. Some babies are just happier and more content than others, whereas some are more fussy and unsettled. Some children are outgoing, while others are more reserved. Your child's personality will affect their overall development, because it moulds the risks they will take, their natural level of tenacity and stubbornness, and their enthusiasm for learning new things.

All areas of development are interconnected

Your child's development doesn't happen in silos. Instead, all areas of your child's development are connected. All the different developmental skills are related to each other, and everything your child practises or learns to do will affect another area of their development. Every new skill learnt has a flow-on or crossover effect in other areas of development, in both positive and negative ways.

For example, when your child learns to reach for and bat something with their hand, this provides the opportunity to learn that their fingers can grasp, that different things feel different and sound different, and that when they bat something it might make a sound (early cause and effect). From this they might also learn to grasp a toy. Grasping and bringing a toy to their mouth enables your child to learn that different things have different textures and flavours. Putting things in their mouth also helps babies and children to learn to move their tongue to different parts of their mouth, to learn to bite down on objects both at the front of their mouth and using the sides of their jaw. This helps your child to learn the tongue, teeth and jaw movements required for eating solids and making sounds.

Another example is when babies and children first start to make sounds. Often, their sound making is unintentional and can take babies by surprise. However, as doting parents, we will often talk back, and take part in a 'baby conversation' with them. As a result, vocalising is helping your baby to recognise that they can gain the attention of others by making noises with their mouths. It also supports understanding that making a noise can get others to do things for them, and that we, as humans, take turns when we are communicating.

In contrast, if your child has trouble communicating their wants and needs, this can have an impact on their social and emotional development because they have more difficulty interacting with others, and can potentially frequently become frustrated because other people around them cannot understand what they are asking for or what is bothering them.

The combinations of interconnections between different areas of your child's development are many and varied. In the following sections, I describe the most common developmental connections to give you a starting point from which to consider your child's needs.

Impact of gross motor development on other areas

The development of gross motor skills can affect other areas as follows:

- Your child's ability to hold their head upright and sit in an upright position has an impact on their ability to use their eyes to look at the world and/or communicate through eye contact or visual gaze, their ability to use their hands effectively for writing or drawing, playing with toys, pressing a switch or using their mouth, throat, tongue and lungs for communication, and their ability to eat and swallow safely.

- The ability to move about or mobilise, whether that be by rolling, creeping on their tummy, bottom shuffling, crawling, walking, riding a bike or pushing or driving a power wheelchair, affects your child's ability to explore the world, teaches choice making because they can choose where they wish to move on the floor without their parent's help, develops the understanding that they can move from A to B to get to a toy (emergence of motivation and sense of independence), and problem solving (for example, when they come across an obstacle in their way, they have to figure out a way around it). The ability to move also has an impact on your child's opportunities for social interaction and communication with others.

- Having a reasonably stable trunk (referred to as core stability) provides your child with a lot of feedback about where their body is in space, and can give them a sense of control over their own self. As a result, a child's level of trunk stability can impact on their behaviour (for example, some children will move excessively to compensate for their lack of awareness of where their body is in space).

The interconnectedness of child development

Impact of fine motor development on other areas

Your child's ability to use their hands independently has an impact on their independence in everyday living activities such as feeding and dressing themselves, personal hygiene activities like wiping after going to the toilet and brushing their teeth, and their ability to demonstrate their cognitive capacity by writing and drawing.

Impact of communication on other areas

The development of communication skills can affect other areas in these ways:

- The ability to communicate their needs and wants affects your child's behaviour. Not being able to get your message across to another person is a distressing and frustrating experience for any of us, and the same goes for your child. An inability to communicate has the potential to cause behavioural challenges for any child, including children with a disability.

- Communication skills also have an impact on your child's social engagement and participation. Humans by nature are social beings. Being able to communicate helps your child interact with other people in their world. However, your child does not need to be able to speak to communicate well – many other devices are available that can support them to communicate their wants, needs, thoughts and ideas that do not require spoken communication.

- The ability to communicate affects our understanding of your child's cognitive skills, or their intellect, which will have an impact on whether or not they are challenged. The condition 'locked-in syndrome' describes the situation in which a person essentially has full paralysis of their body, except for usually their eyes, while still being fully cognitively capable. This is an example where a good communication system can help a person with locked-in syndrome demonstrate their cognitive capacity.

Impact of cognition (thinking skills) on other areas

Developing cognition can also affect other areas:

- A child's level of cognition will have an impact on their ability to explore, problem solve, and learn new skills. In children, lower levels of cognition can be seen in those who have limited play skills – their cognition is affecting their understanding of how they can explore and play with toys.

- A child's cognition will also affect their ability to learn to move and do the activities they need to look after themselves, such as dressing and bathing. Learning to, for example, crawl, walk, and go up and down stairs requires motor planning that will be somewhat impaired in a child who has lower levels of cognition. Similarly, learning to go to the toilet, brush your teeth, and get dressed also requires motor planning, manipulation of objects, and an understanding of the purpose of the activity – as a result, a cognitive impairment will have an impact on the child's ability to learn these skills. This can be seen in children who take much longer to learn a new skill that otherwise would be expected, or have no desire to learn a new skill they need for everyday life.

For Phoebe (who I mentioned in the introduction to this part), and when considering where to start for her development, all areas of her development need to be considered, because all of these will have an impact on another area of her development. The same is true for your child. Considering your child's needs in each of these areas, and how they might be affecting other areas of development, can help you determine your child's strengths and priorities for treatment.

Health and wellbeing trumps all other areas of development

As mentioned earlier in this chapter, health and wellbeing refers to your child's basic physical and mental health needs, which must be

The interconnectedness of child development

maintained at a basic level for your child to be able to learn and develop. Any interruption to their physical or mental health will affect their developmental progress. And this interruption continuing for a long time can have an impact on your child's overall developmental potential. As a result, it is important to always consider your child's underlying physical and mental health – if it is being compromised, the body will naturally focus on improving their physical and mental health first, so issues in these areas will always trump other areas of your child's development.

At a basic level, before any other development can occur, your child's basic physiological needs must be met. This means that your child's basic body systems need to be functioning adequately (breathing, heart rate, blood pressure, digestion and excretion of waste) for optimal improvements in their development to occur. For example, I want you to consider this: if you are hungry because you skipped lunch, how well do you find yourself concentrating at 3 pm? Or if you have not had enough sleep the night before, how well can you concentrate to learn something new the next day? How well can you cope with stress in each of these situations? If you are really cold, how well do you typically interact with others and concentrate? The same applies for children. Many children with developmental difficulties or disabilities have numerous medical challenges going on as part of their condition. They might have difficulty feeding, and so require supplemental feeding. They might have seizures. They might have difficulty controlling their body temperature. They might have pain, which then also affects their sleeping. Every single one of these situations will influence a child's development and learning.

The following figure adapts Maslow's hierarchy of needs, showing your child's fundamental health and wellbeing needs underpin their overall development.

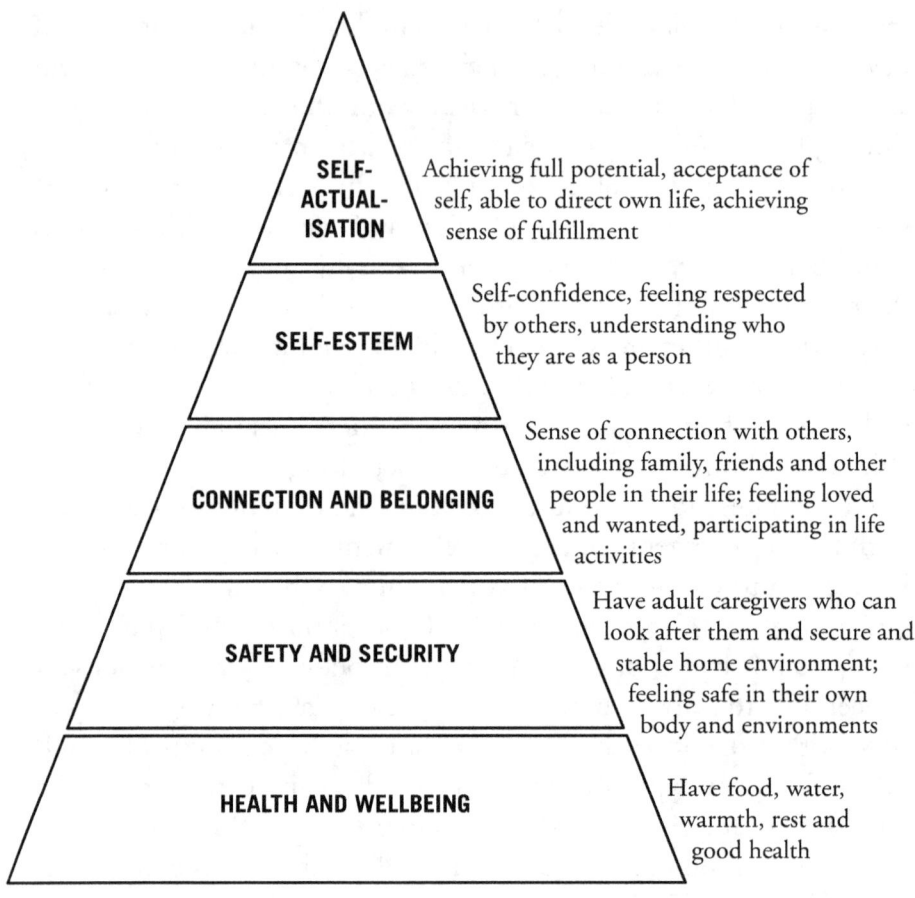

Another fundamental need for children to learn and develop is regulation. Regulation is your child's ability to be alert, engaged and in control of their emotions. Your child needs to feel regulated, or in an optimal mental and emotional state to be able to interact well with their environment and the people and things around them. If your child is feeling anxious, irritated, distressed, upset, or over- or under-stimulated, it will be difficult for them to optimally engage and learn new skills.

The purpose of explaining this model is to help you to understand the underlying physiological processes your child needs to have sorted for them to be in an optimal position to develop. If your

The interconnectedness of child development

child has a heart or lung condition, their body is going to firstly direct its energy and activity towards making sure your child's body has enough blood and oxygen running around their body, rather than on your child's development. If your child is experiencing lots of seizures, their body will be directing its energy and activity towards managing the repercussions of the seizures, rather than your child's development. If your child is not putting on enough weight, or if their growth is not adequate, their body is going to direct all its energy and activity towards helping your child to grow. If your child has trouble regulating their emotions, and experiences moments or even long episodes of distress, that is going to affect their ability to engage, interact, and learn. Or if your child or a child you are caring for has experienced trauma or neglect previously, they might need to develop a sense of stability and confidence that they are being cared for before their development can thrive. Whenever your child has a physical health or emotional health problem or need that is not adequately being addressed, their physical and cognitive development will 'take a back seat' to the overall aim of survival.

It is important to understand this concept for two reasons:

1. It allows you to recognise the importance of always considering and trying to make sure your child's overall wellbeing is as good as it can be. Doing this will help you to be confident that your child's body is in an optimal state to be learning and developing.

2. It also allows you to be aware of potential slowdowns, plateaus or even mild loss of developmental skills when your child is unwell, having seizures, in hospital, having difficulty gaining weight, feeling dysregulated, or any other circumstance in which their basic physiological and psychological needs are not being optimally met. This is not a reflection of you as a parent, and this is not a backwards step for your child. This is purely a reflection of the circumstances of your child's health and wellbeing. Once your child's health and wellbeing needs are again being met, you can expect that your child will return

to their previous level of functioning, and then continue to improve towards their optimal potential. Assuming your child's underlying needs are met within a reasonable time frame, they can 'catch up' on their development and continue to progress towards their full potential.

CHAPTER SEVEN

Understanding your child's development

The previous chapter looked at how each of your child's different areas of development is interconnected. The next step towards helping your child requires you to understand the patterns children tend to follow when they develop, as well as how to understand all the other external variables that influence their development and overall abilities.

This chapter will firstly explore how children typically develop over time, progressing through their developmental skills. The principles covered will enable you to then understand how you can help your child to progress with their development. Secondly, we will explore some models that will help you gain a broader understanding of your child's needs and development within the context of everything else that is going on in their body, life and your wider community – because, ultimately, each of these things may have an impact on their developmental progress and the opportunities available for them to become as happy, confident and independent as possible. By understanding these principles and models, you will better understand how your child is progressing, what other factors might be contributing to them achieving (or not achieving) their optimal development, and functional outcomes, and how you can support your child to develop and become as independent and capable as possible.

How development progresses

Babies and children typically follow certain patterns and processes that underpin the development of new skills. The patterns include developing from the head down, and developing from the trunk out. The processes include the concept of horizontal and vertical development, and the concept of development being a continuous process of acquisition and refinement of skills, in preparation to develop the next skill.

Development of the trunk from the head down

Babies typically develop control of their trunk starting with the head and progressively developing down from there. Control of their head and neck first develops by babies learning to turn their head to each side and hold their head in the middle – first when they are lying on their back, and then when being held upright. Then babies develop control of their upper back, then lower back, then pelvis, then hips. Subsequently, if your child does not have the ability to hold their head upright by themselves, being able to control their pelvis will be more difficult. Instead, they are likely to require external help to hold their pelvis stable, such as supports provided in a chair or a standing frame.

Understanding this pattern of development can help you understand how to support your child with their own development: if your child does not yet know how to control their head in space, it will be difficult for them to learn to use their trunk to sit upright on their own; if your child does not yet know how to hold their trunk upright, it will be difficult for them to learn to use their pelvis and legs effectively to stand up. This is not to say that they won't be able to learn to sit or stand in the long term, and this does not mean that we won't help them to sit and stand in supportive equipment; but it does mean that your child may need to gain or be supported to control the body part above before they can control the body part below.

Development of the trunk from the head down

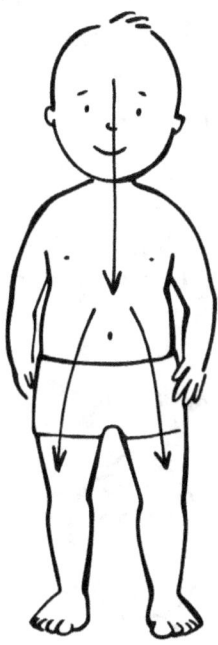

Development from the trunk out

Babies and children also develop from the trunk out. What this means is that babies and children require control of their trunk in order to be able to optimally control their limbs. This is because a strong and stable trunk provides a stable base from which your child can learn to move and control their limbs. You can think of the trunk like the stable base plate of the body – it provides the basic structure and stability of the body, from which all other parts of the body can fix themselves and move off. If the base plate is wobbly (ie: if their trunk is wobbly), it is much harder for your child to accurately and consistently control their reaching, their stepping, and even hold their head in an upright position. The principle of developing from the trunk out also applies to learning to control the limbs. Typically children require reasonable control of their shoulder and elbow before they can optimally control their wrist, hand and fingers for fine manipulative activities such as writing or typing. So, typically, a child begins to control their fingers to manipulate objects only *after* they have developed sufficient trunk control to be able to sit upright, and sufficient control at their shoulder and elbow to successfully do the fine manipulative task such as threading beads, doing up a zipper or button, or drawing with a pencil. So without the ability to sit upright (whether this be independently or through the use of assistive equipment), your child will not have a stable base from which they can move their arms and then wrist and hand and fingers with control.

Development from the trunk out

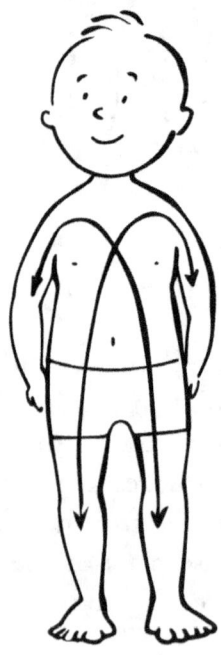

The stability of the trunk also plays an important role in your child's ability to hold their head upright in an optimal position, which in turn affects how they use their eyes to interact and engage with others, and their ability to use their lips, mouth, tongue and throat to speak and to safely swallow food and liquids.

Development from simple to complex

Child development progresses from mastering simple movements or activities before progressing onto more complex movements or activities. This progression from simple to complex occurs in all areas of child development, including motor, communication, and cognitive or thinking skills.

For example, children will first learn to reach their arm out towards a toy to hit it. Once they have mastered that, they will then learn to grasp it and bring that toy to their mouth. And after they have mastered that, they will then learn to use two hands together to manipulate that toy by turning it over, pushing it together or pulling it apart, or poking it with a single finger. When learning to use a pencil, children will progress from doing simple lines and circles, to learning to write letters and words. When following instructions, children will start by learning to respond to their name, and then will start to follow single-step instructions, and then will learn to follow complex multistep instructions.

Posture affects function

In a simplified way, your child's posture is a reflection of their ability to hold their body in an optimal position to do the things they need and want to do in daily life. When talking about posture, people often talk about sitting or standing posture. An optimal sitting posture for developmental purposes often includes an upright head that is in line with the trunk and pelvis, and approximately 90-degree angles at the hips, knees and ankles. An optimal standing posture consists of an upright head that is sitting directly over your child's neck, shoulders, trunk, pelvis and then legs and feet. So why is your child's posture important?

Your child's posture provides the foundational position from which they can then move and complete a task. An optimal posture requires both stability and adaptability. Stability is required to provide that stable base from which your child can move their limbs and head. However, the posture also needs to adapt to the variable requirements of each task.

An optimal posture as the starting point from which your child can then do a task provides three important benefits:

- It usually is energy efficient, which means that it does not take a lot of effort for your child to maintain that position. This energy efficiency is incredibly important for tasks that require your child to hold that posture for a sustained period of time, such as sitting in a chair at a table at school, or standing upright and walking long distances around the community.

- It provides an effective position from which your child can then carry out the activities they need to do. For example, an optimal trunk posture will assist your child stepping up and down stairs, or might assist them to sit independently without using their hands to hold themselves up. Without an optimal posture, your child may fatigue more quickly, or might not be able to successfully complete a task or activity independently.

- It reduces the risk of your child developing complications as a result of a sub-optimal posture. For example, children who persistently sit or stand in a slumped posture are more at risk for developing contractures, or postural deformities such as scoliosis. These secondary changes can have a further impact on their ability to function and move to the best of their ability, and for some children can also contribute to pain and other medical complications.

Putting it all together: Developmental principles and your child

Understanding the principles of head-down and trunk-out developmental patterns, simple to complex learning, and the impact of posture on function can help you to decide how you can help your own child with their developmental progress:

- To help your child improve their head control, you can make sure they are well supported and aligned in their trunk; that is, their head is positioned right on top of their shoulders, trunk and pelvis. This gives your child the best chance of learning to control their head in the midline.

- If your child does not have very good control of their head or trunk, providing them with external supports to help hold them steady will be important when you are teaching them to use their arms or legs. Your child ideally needs to have a stable trunk in order to use their arms and legs effectively.

- You can take steps to help your child to stabilise their trunk. This will give them more opportunity to better control their head, arms and legs. And stabilising the trunk can come organically by improving their core strength and stability, or from external supports such as your hands, braces and supportive equipment.

When setting goals and choosing activities for your child to practise, understanding that your child needs to progress from simple to complex will allow you to choose goals or activities that are slightly more challenging than what they are currently achieving, but not beyond their current capability. For example, if your child is learning to use their hands to hold toys and objects, they will need to progress from holding large objects in the palm of their hand to grasping smaller objects between their fingertips. By understanding this progression, you can be more confident that your child might achieve success with the goal or activity, helping to boost your child's self-confidence and also prevent frustration for both you and your child.

Understanding vertical and horizontal development

When health professionals talk about the 'vertical' development of your child, we're not talking about how tall they are. Instead, we're referring to the sequence of skills that your child learns over time in any one position. So, for example, a baby and child's upright skills will develop from not being able to hold their head up, to being able to hold their head up, being able to take weight through their feet with a parent helping, being able to stand by themselves and then to walking.

'Horizontal' development, on the other hand, refers to the series of skills that your child is learning at any one time. So, for example, at four months of age, children are typically learning to hold their head upright when placed in sitting position and when on their tummy, learning to push up through their forearms when on their tummy, to lift their hands to their feet and their feet to their mouths when on their back, and to accurately reach and grasp a toy. Your baby learning to do each of these different skills will support the development of the other skills your baby is learning to do at this point in time, and in the future.

The concept of vertical and horizontal development helps you to understand different ways you can help your child to progress in their development of skills. At any single point in time, you can help your child to work on all the different skills from a horizontal development perspective. Alternatively, you can also choose to work on easier skills or harder skills within the vertical development perspective, which is outlined in more detail in the following section.

Development as a continual process

Development is a continual process:

- The activity of yesterday prepared me for the activity of today.
- The activity of today is preparing me for the activity of tomorrow.
- The activity of tomorrow will refine the activity of today.

Every movement, skill or activity your child is currently learning is preparing them to be able to do something new in the future. And every movement, skill or activity your child is practising today is helping them to refine a movement, skill or activity they have already learnt. New skills are constantly being laid down on top of previous skills, and previous skills provide a foundation from which your child can learn new skills. Different skills are emerging and evolving over time as your child learns and masters new movements, activities or skills.

This principle is important to understand. As discussed in chapter 4, even if your child is seemingly repeating a task that they have already mastered, they are still improving and refining that skill, and getting ready for a new skill. In *Outliers*, author Malcolm Gladwell outlines that learning a new skill takes 10,000 hours of practice – your child repeatedly practising the same movement or activity is helping them to gain mastery over that skill. And mastery enables your child to be able to perform that new skill in different environments and under different conditions, with much more speed and efficiency, and without as much concentration as when they first learned the skill. This is then preparing your child to be ready to learn the next skill. This same principle applies to anyone learning a new skill, such as learning to play an instrument – the more practice we get, the more we can refine our skills, which then enables us to play more and more difficult musical pieces.

Let's look at a practical example. In preparation for learning how to sit, a child will be learning and refining skills such as holding their head upright, propping on their outstretched arms when lying on their tummy, tucking their chin in when lying on their tummy, and bringing their hands to their feet when lying on their back. All of these activities are giving your child the necessary skills to be able to sit up. When they learn how to sit, the activity of sitting is helping them to prepare for activities such as crawling and walking (by holding their head and trunk upright, by rotating their trunk, and by shifting their weight from side to side). And after learning to sit, a child will learn to crawl on hands and knees, pull up onto their knees, and eventually pull to stand. Each of these activities will help to refine and improve the child's ability to sit by allowing them to be able to reach further outside of their base of support, sit with a more mature posture, and transition into and out of a variety of different sitting positions.

Capturing the complexity of your child's development

The principles and processes discussed in this chapter and within this part of the book aim to help you understand that all of your child's needs are interconnected, and how they are interconnected. However, you may still be feeling a bit overwhelmed by how to use this information to make decisions about where to focus your efforts to help your child.

In this section, we will explore two models that are commonly used to understand disability in the context of everything else in life.

The ICF model

The International Classification of Functioning, Disability and Health (ICF) is a model that was developed and endorsed by the World Health Organization. The ICF model captures the complexity of human functioning and the impact of health and disability on an individual's functioning in the context of everything else within a person's life and environment. The ICF provides a framework that I can almost guarantee your child's doctors and therapists will be using when they are working with you and your child. So naturally it would be helpful for you, as a parent, to understand this model as well, and the language and concepts drawn from it. You can then use the ICF framework to explore your child's development and functioning from many different lenses or focuses, and to help you decide on the different areas to focus on to help your child to progress and lead their best life.

The ICF model (shown in the following figure) comprises six components, which are all interconnected and influence on each other, as demonstrated by the interconnecting arrows.

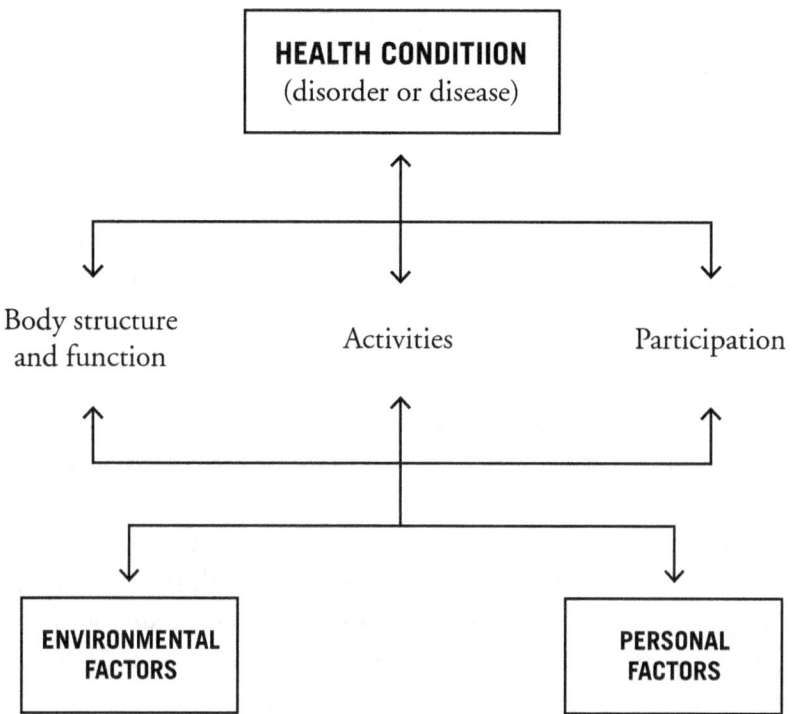

At the top of the model is the health condition or disability, demonstrating that this will impact and influence the three components below.

The three middle components consist of body structure and function, activities, and participation:

- *Body structure and function* refers to your child's actual body parts and how they work. So this might include your child's muscles, bones, nerves, eyes and other sensory systems, and their internal organs. When considering your child's body structure and function, you might know that they have weakness in specific muscles, that they cannot feel a part of their body very well, that they have one leg shorter than the other, that they have a joint contracture at their elbow, or they have a deformity such as leg that bows or a missing limb.

- *Activities* describe the tasks, actions or activities that your child does in their everyday life. This might include standing up, sitting down, rolling over, getting dressed, brushing their teeth, writing, eating and drinking, and washing themselves.
- *Participation* describes being involved in and actively participating in a life situation. For your child, this might mean being a member of your family, attending school, participating in social or competitive sports, attending scouts, visiting friends of family, going shopping or going out for dinner.

Each of these three middle components influence and interact with each other. So, for example, if your child is unable to participate in a school activity such as playing with their peers, this could be as a result of difficulties related to one of the three components. And vice versa – if your child has a problem with their leg strength, that might affect their ability to go up and down stairs, which then might affect their participation because they cannot visit their best friend at their house because it is only accessed via stairs.

The bottom two components are environment and personal factors. These two components are linked back to the three middle components because they both will influence your child's overall performance and abilities:

- *Environmental factors* describe the environments your child is in or those around your child. Your child's environments might include their home environment, their day care/kindy or school environment, and their community environment such as the local shops, parks and playgrounds, libraries, restaurants and footpaths – any physical or social environment in your community.
- *Personal factors* describe your child's individual factors, unrelated to their health condition or diagnosis but which still might impact on their abilities. This might include their personality, their height and weight, their age, ethnicity, family, and other social and economic factors.

So why is understanding the ICF model useful?

The ICF model is useful in helping you understand the breadth of your child's needs, how all of these needs impact on each other, and also the different areas or components where you can intervene to help your child. In addition, it also provides you with a common language when communicating with your child's healthcare team, enabling you to be more clear with them about your goals for your child, and empowering you to be able to advocate for your child's needs with health professionals, funding agencies, and other support agencies you meet along the way.

Case study

Melinda is a little girl with a high-level spina bifida. This means that she has a form of spinal cord injury that impacts on her muscle activation, muscle strength, and sensation below the level of her spina bifida, which is high up on her back. We can use the ICF in two ways for Melinda:

- We can use it to explore and break down all the different areas that her disability affects in the middle three components. If using the ICF model to explore the different areas of impact, my preference is to consider a child's participation first and work my way backwards. So when considering Melinda's participation, we can say she is very social and can socially engage with others, but her physical participation in activities with her peers is limited by her physical disability and she requires the support of her parents and carers. When considering her activities, we can say that she can roll over from back to tummy and tummy to back, she can move herself from lying to sitting, and she can sit independently. When considering her body structures and functions, we can say that she has decreased sensation in her arms and legs and trunk, weakness of the muscles of her arms and legs and trunk, a contracture of one of her joints in her arm, and a mild scoliosis.

- We can also then consider which environmental and personal factors are influencing on her overall abilities. So, for Melinda, her social personality is a strength that supports her participation and play with her friends, but her stubborn streak when she doesn't want to do something she does not like can make it difficult to challenge her physical abilities during therapy or when out in social situations. When considering the environment, Melinda's community is affecting her ability to play with her friends because she requires disability access to the environments in which her friends play (such as parks, playgrounds and the local library), and some of these environments actually prohibit Melinda's participation.

Once we have identified all the potential components that have an impact on Melinda's abilities, we can then consider which components, if improved, are going to assist to progress her abilities. This will help Melinda's parents and therapists decide which components to address during therapy, how to prioritise where her therapies or interventions might be best delivered, and what environmental factors we can addresss in order to make the most impact in her life. Considering each aspect of her development, this might involve a combination of interventions or supports.

In Melinda's case, her therapy supports or interventions might include identifying accessible community locations where she can play with her friends (environment), sourcing a power wheelchair to give Melinda more independent mobility so she can participate in physical activities with her friends (activity and participation), and also providing a wrist splint to straighten her wrist slightly so that she can better use her hands to play (body structure and function).

'Nature versus nurture' and the ICF model

The 'nature versus nurture' debate looks at whether a child's abilities are in-built – that is, they are set from birth (nature) – or related to their lived experiences and opportunities (nurture). In my experience, and considering the concept of the ICF, I think it is a bit of both. People are born with certain genetic traits or aptitudes that mean they are naturally better at certain tasks. My husband is naturally a better runner than me – he has long, lean legs, and has a physiological make up more suited for speed, whereas I have shorter, stockier legs, with a physiological make up more suited for long distance. However, our genetic traits and aptitudes only get us so far, and it is our experiences and opportunities and what we do with those opportunities that affect our overall abilities and functioning.

The same applies for your child with a disability. They were born with a certain condition or genetic make up, and we can't do anything to change that. However, if we maximise their experiences and opportunities, they can make the most of their abilities. When considering the ICF model, the nature view would cover their personal factors and their body structure and functions, whereas the nurture view covers the environmental factors and their participation.

Adding six important 'F-words' to the ICF model

No, I am not about to start using swear words, I promise!

The F-words of childhood disability are part of a concept that builds upon the ICF model, and provides a different way of considering the aspects of life that are meaningful and important to childhood and development for children with disabilities. These F-words, and what they encompass, are as follows:

- *Function:* This is all the things that children do, focusing on what they can do; how they do them is not important.
- *Family:* Family is the essential 'environment' or social circumstance that all children grow up in.

- *Fitness:* This refers to how the children stay physically active and participate in physical activities, including both exercise and other physical recreational activities.
- *Fun:* This refers to the specific activities children enjoy doing and taking part in.
- *Friends:* This refers to the friendships and social connections that children develop, which is an essential part of a child developing a sense of who they are.
- *Future:* This refers to the child's and their parent's expectations and hopes and dreams for the future.

These six F-words can help you (and your child's health and therapy team) think about what is important to your child, to their overall development and to their future and find a balance by ensuring all areas are addressed.

See the 'Further reading' section for resources that provide more information in this area.

Social model of disability

The social model of disability recognises that the barriers that are present in our environment – which include physical barriers, social policy barriers and the attitudes of others – are the primary contributors to someone experiencing disability. This model considers the physical disability to be just one of many different human experiences, and moves away from positioning a person's disability as something that needs to be fixed or improved for that person to be able to participate within our society. Instead, the model argues our society and environments need to adapt to enable all humans, regardless of their abilities or disabilities, to participate.

So, for example, instead of a person with a disability having to learn to walk up and down steps in order to access a building in our community, the social model of disability suggests that the building (in fact, all buildings) should be made accessible for all. By making every building accessible, we are accommodating for everyone – for example, parents with prams, parents with small children who cannot yet go up and down stairs, elderly people with painful arthritis, or the young person who has broken their leg and is currently using crutches to get around – not just people with a disability.

As you can see, many factors will have an impact on your child's potential to learn to move and play to the best of their ability, and also on their potential to do what they want to in life. Some of these factors will involve you helping and supporting your child to be the best they can be, physically and cognitively. And other factors will involve considering your child's personality, the physical and social environments you live in, the opportunities for development that your child may be able to access and participate in, and also what you or your child wants and dreams for. My feeling is that considering all the different types of factors that will have an impact on your child's potential and development, and making sure you are addressing all the relevant areas at any one time, is the best approach to helping your child to lead their best life.

CHAPTER EIGHT

Identifying your child's strengths and prioritising needs

Having developed a broader understanding of your child's needs across all areas, you can now focus on where it is you want to start helping your child to develop and be the best they can be. The first step here is learning to recognise and place value on your child's strengths. You can then explore prioritising your child's needs, by looking at what is important versus what is urgent, understanding how to prioritise the important needs, and setting goals or deciding on focus areas that are meaningful and measurable.

Recognising your child's strengths

So far in the chapters in this part, we have focused a lot on your child's needs and their differences. In this section, I want to switch gears and focus on your child's strengths. Every child has strengths and talents, but these can sometimes get lost in among all the time and attention we spend on identifying your child's needs. Your child's strengths are immeasurably valuable to understand. In fact, I often think they are even more important to understand than their needs. Using your child's strengths can have a powerful impact on their overall outcomes (that is, achieving their best and becoming confident and fulfilled).

A quote often attributed to Albert Einstein argues, 'Everybody is a genius. But if you judge a fish by its ability to climb a tree, it will live its whole life believing it is stupid.' Although no evidence exists that Einstein actually said this, the sentiment remains. So much of your journey with your child within this book has been focused on identifying their needs. But every person has strengths – things they are good at, things they find come easily to them, things they enjoy and are drawn to doing. And strengths play an important part in helping us to understand our value and self-worth. As humans, we often subconsciously make decisions about our lives that play to our strengths. Even as children. As you were growing up, if numbers and maths came easily to you and were something you excelled at, you've likely chosen a career or job that plays to these strengths, such as an accountant, engineer, or a cash register operator. Alternatively, if you found words and comprehension more difficult, you are unlikely to have chosen to become an author, a historian, or an English teacher. If you are naturally creative and artistic, it often follows that you choose a career that plays to that strengths. If you are good with your hands and good at making things, you are likely to follow a career in that path. This can even play out in the home – if you're good with numbers but not with your hands, perhaps you focus on the family budget, but don't get involved in the kitchen renovation.

And what would it be like if you were asked to do something that was not playing to your strengths? How would that feel? Doing things we are not familiar with and not naturally good at often leads to us feeling slow, confused, frustrated, disappointed in our inabilities, and lost. We may question our abilities, question our self-worth, and feel quite down about ourselves.

Playing to their strengths is something that often comes naturally to parents of typically developing children. If a child is interested and passionate about dancing and singing, parents will often put their child into classes or activities that will help them to follow that strength and passion. If a child is very meticulous and precise, the parent is likely to choose toys and activities that play to that strength, because as a parent we know that the child will enjoy the activity and grow from it. Getting the child to participate in activities that they do not find come naturally and do not enjoy is harder, for parents and the child. Most parents will understand how hard it is to get your child to read is if they do not like reading and find it difficult.

So it seems almost a bit perplexing that we seem to do the opposite for children with developmental difficulties or disabilities. So much of the life of a child with developmental delays or disabilities is focused on discovering the things they cannot do or have difficulty with, and then helping them get better at these things they are not naturally good at. As therapists, we are often asked about what toys or activities we would recommend a family purchases for their child's birthday or for Christmas because the family wants to purchase activities that will help their child develop their skills. And for children with conditions such as autism, who have very strong strengths in narrow areas, such as 'being obsessed' with trains or dinosaurs, or being very structured in their processes and habits, parents are often tempted to avoid that particular strength in an attempt to expand their interest repertoire, or to help them to better cope with the opposite of their natural tendencies, such as helping the child to cope with lack of structure and change.

While I don't mean to say that we should just ignore the difficulties your child experiences, I do believe that, instead of looking at them as problems, we should celebrate your child's strengths, and enhance and harness them to help your child to improve.

Your child's strengths provide a great opportunity for motivation, for the development of independence, and for the development of self-identity. What makes your child unique? What are they drawn to? What do they find easy? What are they good at, without even trying? What keeps their attention the longest?

To help you discover your child's strengths further, try the following:

- Consider their physical and cognitive abilities, relationships with others and their interests and habits. What do they thrive on? What lights them up?
- Keep a strengths journal to help you keep track of everyday observations. Do they become enthralled every time music is played? This might mean music and rhythm is a strength. Do they enjoy looking at the pictures in the junk mail or in shopping brochures? This might mean your child is strong with symbols and pictures.
- Do lots of different activities together, and watch your child's behaviours in each situation you try. You can then use those behaviours to help discover what their strengths are. Do they gravitate towards other children? This might indicate they have a strength and interest for interacting and social situations. Do they prefer physically active situations over more sedentary activities? This might indicate they have physical strengths.

Keep in mind also that different types of strengths are possible, including:

- personal strengths
- social-interactive strengths
- emotional and coping strengths
- physical strengths and abilities
- self-care strengths (looking after themselves)
- language strengths
- logic and problem-solving strengths.

By understanding each of these strengths, you can take advantage of them and enhance them to help your child develop their sense of competence and self-worth. You can also leverage your child's strengths to help them to improve on other areas that they find more difficult. For example, if your child is quite practical and hands on, but struggles with understanding written letters and language, you might take advantage of that practical strength by using LEGO bricks with letters or words on them and then asking your child to put together the letters to spell words, or alternatively put together the words to form sentences. Your child will be using their strength of practical construction to learn about their letters and words.

Let your child lead

I focus on developing self-identity and competence in much more detail in part IV, but for now remember the following: resist the urge to compare your child's strengths against the abilities of others or against your expectations. Your child's strengths might not actually be the activities they find the easiest. If you only consider the things your child is good at, you are likely to miss some strengths that you might not have yet noticed, or that might be more subtle. You can always (and I would encourage you to!) help your child to improve their strengths areas, because this will give them a huge sense of pride and value.

Let your child follow their passions – let your child make choices about what they spend their time doing. Developing a passion allows your child to develop their identity of themselves outside of their disability. A great example of this is actress, performer and dancer Kiruna Stamell, who is also a host on Australia's *Playschool*, and a person of short stature (or a person with dwarfism). Kiruna is a strong, capable woman who was able to follow her passion and forge a career as an actress, without playing one-dimensional characters. Zach Anner is another example. His parents allowed him to pursue his goals of becoming a comedian, TV producer and writer, which allowed him to forge his career and develop his identity – as someone with desires, dreams, aspirations, goals, interests, relationships, purpose, and meaning.

Prioritising needs

Once you have an understanding of your child's strengths and needs, for some parents, the list that they are left with can be somewhat overwhelming. You know what your child needs, but where should you start?

It is at this stage that you need to spend some time thinking about how to prioritise your child's needs.

Considering what is urgent and what is important

Urgent tasks are things that need to be done imminently. Important tasks are things that need to be done and will make a big difference to your child's future, but are not necessarily urgent. Urgency and importance can be considered along a continuum, and tasks can become more urgent or more important, or less urgent or important over time or at different stages in your child's life.

However, a common mistake is to focus on only what seems urgent, instead of what seems important. We can get caught up in the day-to-day tasks of attending therapy, working on your child's current skills and looking at the skills they need right now, and miss out on thinking about the bigger picture for your child and their life. This frequently happens when children are approaching the commencement of school. In a child's early years of life, parents commonly focus on the most obvious or urgent needs for their child. For example, their child might not be able to crawl or walk, so parents will focus lots of time and therapy on helping their child learn to move. Perhaps the same child can adequately get their message across to their parents and people familiar with them, so communication is overlooked. Or their child can move adequately around the family home by crawling or using a walker, so the parents do not think they need a wheelchair. However, as the saying goes, 'the days are long but the years are short' – and before they know it, their child is only a year away from starting school, and all of a sudden the child urgently needs to be able to communicate better with others and/or get around the school independently, but only have a short amount of time to work on these important skills. The same thing can occur when a child is transitioning from attending school to finishing school and finding meaningful activities or employment to engage in after school. Their needs will change, and suddenly what was important becomes less important, and what was not urgent becomes more urgent.

Hopefully, by this stage of reading this book, you will have spent some time thinking about your child's needs across all areas of their development, considering what their future function or future difficulties might be, and understanding their needs within the context of their life. As a result, you will hopefully also find considering what is urgent and what is important much easier than when you first opened this book. However, my recommendation is to consider this distinction on a regular basis. How regular might depend upon your child and the extent of their needs, but a review every few months is a good start. This allows you to switch your focus to taking a broad look at your child's needs across all areas and within the context of what is happening in their life, both now and in the future, and spending some time considering the important and urgent things that need to get done. By doing this, no developmental stage or transition should come by surprise and you should hopefully feel as prepared as you possibly can for each upcoming activity or developmental stage in your child's life.

For help with deciding what tasks are urgent and which are important, consider the following:

- your child's needs

- your child's strengths, and your and their hopes and wishes for the future

- your child's, your personal, and your family values (see the chapters in part V for more information on how to do this)

- your child's current needs, across all areas of their development (refer to chapters 6 and 7), and in combination with their future function and needs, across all areas of their development (refer to the chapters in part I)

- any future difficulties or transitions such as starting school, finishing school, the arrival of a new sibling (refer to part I).

You can then use the following chart to plot your child's needs in terms of urgency versus importance. Tasks that are urgent and important are placed in the top right of the chart, for example, and are completed first. Urgent but not as important tasks are completed next and so on.

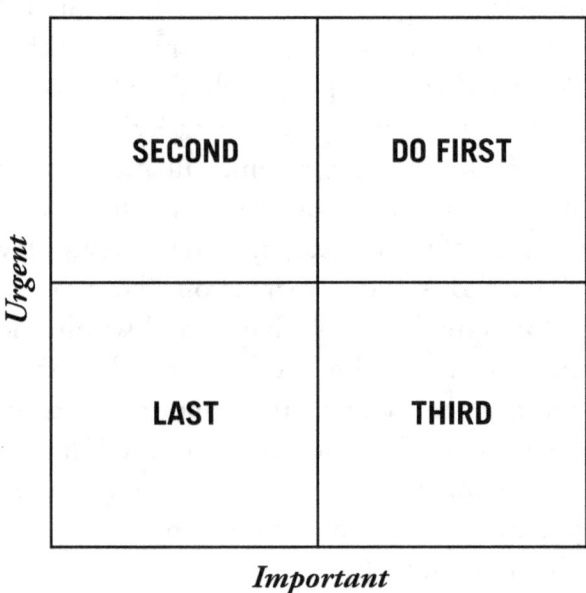

When plotting your child's needs, keep in mind the following:

- The urgency and importance of tasks is going to vary, depending on factors such as time, the importance of the activity or need to you, your child's and your family's beliefs and values (more on this in part V), and the circumstances of your child's life, including transitions such as starting school, finishing school and moving house.
- Consider whether you can group any of the needs into focus areas. Do any similarities exist in areas of need? Do any of

the tasks fall into a shared group with a shared goal or shared developmental area?

- Use the areas or groups of need you have identified to develop goals or focus areas for your child's supports.

Setting goals (or not setting goals)

Setting goals is a reasonably natural part of the therapy process. Goals are used by parents, therapists and funding agencies to help everyone involved in your child's care work towards a concrete aim or improvement. In particular, funding agencies will use goals and the achievement (or lack thereof) of those goals to justify whether or not the funding your child is receiving should be extended or continued.

I personally feel a bit torn about the idea of setting goals for children – let me explain why. I have two children who are typically developing. I have never attended a GP or speech therapy appointment with my child and been asked, 'What are your goals for your child?' If I were, my response would probably be something vague like, 'For him to be happy and healthy', or 'For her to have friends and enjoy and find meaning in her life'. Both of these examples are not particularly concrete. If you ask this question to parents of children with developmental delays or disability, outside of the context of therapy appointments, I suspect they would answer similarly. Ultimately, our goals for our children are the same; it is just that our children may take different pathways to achieve the same life 'goal' or purpose.

However, as soon as you have a parent in a therapy situation, they are likely to be frequently asked about their goals for their child. Why do we approach this so differently for children with a disability? Maybe we shouldn't.

Another problem with pushing to set goals for children is that we are focusing on the things they can't do that we would like them to be able to do. The focus is still on the differences and difficulties, rather than on the strengths and abilities. Often the goal is worded something like, 'For Rasheed to be able to walk independently', or 'For Sailor to be able to write her name'. And if the goal is not achieved, what does that mean? Does it mean the child has failed?

Does it mean that they will never achieve that goal or they just need more time? Does it mean continuing to work towards that goal is pointless and instead we should focus on something else? Of course, the child hasn't failed and continuing is not pointless.

For this reason, I believe that deciding on focus areas for treatment, rather than setting goals, is much more beneficial. But because the goal was set in such a concrete way, there is a possibility it might feel that way.

Focus areas

Focus areas can be considered broad areas of your child's development that you would like them to improve on. For example, you might choose to focus on improving your child's gross motor skills, or your child's interaction with others. Unlike the specific goals referred to in the preceding section, focus areas are more open ended, and allow for exploration of how your child will improve. The outcome seen as a result of improvements in that focus area can be much broader.

The nice thing about setting focus areas is you can choose to also set goals within that focus area if you wish. For example, you might set the goals of 'For Rasheed to be able to move independently on the floor' and 'For Rasheed to be able to stand with assistance' under the focus area of 'improving gross motor skills'.

Setting focus areas or goals that are meaningful and measurable

Regardless of whether you decide to set focus areas or specific goals for your child's development, writing goals that are meaningful and measurable is important. A key strategy here is focusing on function and participation:

- *Function:* An activity that a person does in everyday life. Functional activities include things like walking and running, brushing your hair or teeth, getting dressed, writing with a pencil, tying your shoelaces, or communicating with others.

- *Participation:* The action of taking part in something. Participation might include playing with friends, playing a sport, taking part in activities at school with friends and peers, or visiting and taking part in community activities.

When first discussing goals with parents and families, the goals commonly mentioned are a little like this:

- 'I want my child to improve their core strength and their coordination.'
- 'I want my child to improve their gross and fine motor skills.'
- 'I want my child to improve their behaviour and attention.'

'Why? For what purpose?'

While these goals may be absolutely relevant to the child's needs, they are not particularly meaningful or measurable – because they do not include reference to function or participation. To make these goals more meaningful and measurable, it is useful to ask yourself the question, 'Why?' or 'For what purpose?'

In the case of 'improving core strength and coordination', it would be useful to think about the following questions:

- For what purpose does your child need to improve their core strength and coordination?
- What activities are they having trouble with as a result of their poor core strength and coordination?
- What would be the benefits if your child had better core strength and coordination? What activities could they do that they cannot do now?

In this example, the functional purpose for improving your child's core strength and coordination might be so they can:

- learn to swim and participate in swimming lessons
- play on the playground with their friends or siblings

- learn to sit up better and use their hands for play
- sit still with a good posture during meal times
- learn to throw and catch a ball so they can start playing a sport
- learn to ride a bike with their brother or sister.

Each of these new or updated goals focus on the functional activity to improve, and the participation outcome as a result of being able to do that functional activity. Writing goals in this way has three key benefits:

1. They are more meaningful to your child and family because the goal has a purpose and a context.
2. They provide a broader opportunity for more solutions to be explored to achieve the goal.
3. They are more measurable.

I discuss these three aspects in more detail in the following sections.

Meaningful

How excited and motivated do you think your child would be if you said to them, 'Today we are going to help you work on your core strength and coordination'? Not very?! Compare that with, 'Today we are going to help you to learn to throw and catch a ball so you can play with your friends'.

Setting goals that have a purpose and focus on the child's function and participation make the goals real, personal, tangible and meaningful for your child, and also for your family.

You can see that each of the goals in the preceding list includes a context, an environment or a setting for your child to achieve their goal. Having a context for the goal provides concrete and tangible expectations for which situations or environments you hope that goal to be achieved in.

Opportunity for more solutions

Improving core strength and coordination is not really a goal – it could more accurately be described as a treatment strategy that can help your child to achieve their functional goals. However, it is only one strategy of many that could be used to improve a child's functional goals.

For example, if the reason your family would like your child to improve their core strength and coordination is because you would like your child to be able to sit upright and use their hands for play, addressing their core strength and coordination through exercises is only looking at *one* of the possible options available that can help them to achieve their functional goal. Alternatively, when the goal is 'For my child to sit upright and use their hands for play', you can also consider introducing adaptive or supportive equipment, along with positioning and posture strategies, and supportive garments to help them with their motor control. You could also work on their hand function and play skills. Each of these activities will still be working towards the ultimate goal of 'For my child to sit upright and use their hands for play', but you have many more options you can use to meet that goal that would have otherwise been missed. And so the outcome of the goal is also likely to be better.

Measurable

If we set a goal of 'improving core strength and coordination', determining if and when that has been achieved is difficult because there is no clear outcome or endpoint.

In contrast, if the goal is 'to learn to throw and catch a ball', you will very easily know when your child has achieved that – they have achieved it when they can throw and catch a ball!

Alternatively, if your child's goal is 'to learn to climb on the playground', when your child can climb on the playground you know that they have achieved that goal and it is time to move onto a new one.

Why are functional goals important?

Having measurable goals that demonstrate that your child is improving in their function is so important when dealing with agencies that help to fund your child's therapy (more on the options for funding at the end of the book). Most funding agencies or schemes, whether they are government funding, insurance funding, or charity or philanthropic funding, require you to demonstrate the value and achievements being made through the therapies your child is attending.

Consequently, the way your child's goals are worded is an extremely important factor in to whether or not you will be able to prove the benefits of your child's therapy, and therefore receive ongoing funding for ongoing improvements. By focusing on your child's function and participation, you are giving yourself, your child, and your child's therapists the best shot at getting the supports your child needs to develop to the best of their abilities.

CHAPTER NINE

Getting the help you need

A challenging hurdle that parents can sometimes struggle with is actually getting the help you or your child needs. You might now be developing an understanding of what your child's needs are – but where do you go from here? A multitude of different professionals, service providers, approaches to treatment, and funding options are available, and understanding who you should see and how you might get funding to see them can be hard. This chapter aims to help demystify some of the language and information around different types or approaches of professionals and service providers so that you can select the ones that feel right and will benefit your child and family.

Choosing service providers

As part of your child's initial diagnosis and their continuing treatment and reassessment, you're likely to come into contact with a large number of doctors, medical specialists, allied health professionals and early intervention workers. These could include any of the following, and more:

- general practitioners
- paediatricians
- neurologists
- rehabilitation physicians or paediatricians
- eye specialists (ophthalmologists and optometrists)
- physiotherapists
- occupational therapists
- speech pathologists
- social workers
- psychologists
- community-based nurses
- early developmental or early childhood teachers.

Each of these possible professionals or service providers, and their role in your child's treatment, are covered in more detail in appendix C. The list provided there can help you to understand what role each of the health professionals might play in the care of your child, and can help you match the type of professional with the needs of your child.

Each profession has a different focus on what they help with or how they help children, and some crossover can occur between different professions. For example, you might have both a GP and a paediatrician working together to support your child's medical needs. Alternatively you might have a physio and an occupational therapist (OT) assisting your child to learn to use a switch. The speech pathologist then might also join the physio and OT to help learn about switches for communication. As a parent, understanding 'who's who in the zoo' and who does what for your child can be somewhat confusing.

Importantly, your child's individual doctors and therapists will usually never work in isolation. Ideally, your child's medical team and allied health team will work together and maintain high levels of communication with one another. You can see that each doctor and therapist involved has a specific area of expertise that they bring to your child's care, and that it is only by combining these various areas of expertise and having everyone working together that you can ensure your child is receiving the highest level of care across all of their needs.

Of course, choosing a health professional or service provider for your child involves more than just picking out the profession. Here are five more factors to consider when choosing a health professional or service provider for your child:

1. *Choose someone you trust:* Working with a health professional or service provider ideally involves open communication and honesty, so that you know exactly what is happening for your child, and also so that the health professional is supporting you the best they can. Being open and honest requires a level of trust, and this trust can also help you work more collaboratively because you can both be on the same page. Having trust in your child's health professionals or service providers is essential when working towards the best outcomes for your child and family.

2. *Choose someone who gives you all the information you need to feel confident and empowered:* Any health professional or service provider you work with should help you to be as informed and educated and empowered as possible so that you can advocate for your child. Ideally, your health professional should be educating you constantly about your child's needs and teaching you and empowering you to be able to support your child.

3. *Choose someone who has an approach to treatment that feels right for your child and family:* Different therapies and service providers will potentially have different approaches to how they work with children and families. It is important to find health professionals and service providers whose approach to treatment

feels like it is right for you and your child. The approach to treatment will incorporate things like the health professional's personality, the types of treatment they do and how they are applied, as well as their philosophies and values they and their service hold around working with children with developmental delays or disabilities.

4. *Choose someone who has similar values to you and your family, or whose service values resonate with you:* If you are not sure about what your personal or family values are (or how to articulate them), don't stress, we cover this in more detail in part V. For now, remember that, when it comes to choosing a health professional or service provider, this may be someone you end up spending a lot of time with, over many years, and having quite open and honest conversations. As a result, it is important that you feel like your child's health professional or service provider understand and respect your general values and what is important to you and your family.

5. *Choose someone else for a second opinion if the professional or service provider doesn't feel right:* Similar to when you are first getting help to identify your child's needs early, if you are seeing a health professional or service provider and it doesn't feel right to you, don't hesitate to seek out a second opinion or the help of a different service provider.

Choosing a health professional or service provider also brings up funding considerations while accessing treatment. See appendix D for more information on these options in Australia.

Approaches to early intervention

Different service providers may adopt different approaches to how they deliver early intervention services. Depending on the needs of your child and family, you might find that one approach suits your needs better. Some of the approaches can be somewhat similar, and many crossover in the fundamental principles that underlie the approach. However, it is important to understand what the approaches are so that you can find a health professional or service provider whose approach matches the needs of your child and family.

Family-centred care

Almost every early intervention service will (or should) adopt a family-centred approach. Family-centred care recognises that parents and families know their child best, and that your child with a disability exists and functions within the context of your family. This means any services, interventions and supports also fit in within your family context. Family-centred care aims to empower parents and family members in the care of their child.

Child-centred care

While child-centred care can be similar to family-centred care, the difference is that the child is at the centre of the team of support people. They revolve around the child, and the child's needs are central and considered the priority when making decisions about the child's needs.

Case study

Let's look at a case study to better understand the difference between family-centred and child-centred care. Say a child with a rare congenital disability requires therapy to help them to learn to move and play. The child's parents both work – Dad full-time, and Mum part-time. The child also has two older siblings who are school-aged, and who also participate in after-school sports. It is recommended that the child would benefit from receiving intensive therapy to help them learn to use their hands for reaching and grasping. However, to be able to attend this therapy, the mum would have to take a few hours off work each afternoon to take the child to therapy before then picking the siblings up from school. Using a family-centred approach, the therapist would recognise the importance of the child's therapy fitting in around the rest of the family, and so would work with the family to find an alternative way to ensure the child can receive the same level of care without interrupting the family functioning. Alternatively, using a child-centred approach, the child's needs would be made a priority, and the child would receive the therapy regardless of how it interrupted the family routine.

There is no right or wrong approach in terms of whether you choose child-centred care or family-centred care. In fact, there can be some overlap within the two approaches, and the approach you adopt for your child and family will likely change depending on the circumstances of your child's needs at the time. For example, if your child requires an operation on their hips, a child-centred approach might be more appropriate because the child's needs have to come first in this situation. However, when it comes to your child's ongoing therapy, it might be better for you as a family to use a more family-centred approach so that your child's needs fit in with everything else in your family's life.

Multidisciplinary care

Multidisciplinary care involves multiple healthcare professionals supporting different aspects of your child's care. A multidisciplinary healthcare team for a child with a developmental delay or disability might include a paediatrician, physiotherapist, occupational therapist, speech pathologist, dietician and teacher, or any combination of these or other services and supports depending on the child's needs. These professionals will provide intervention primarily focusing on their area of expertise; however, they will still work collaboratively with you and the other health professionals to ensure your child's care is coordinated. This model of care can be useful if your child has quite complex needs, and requires the specific expertise of a number of different health professionals.

Transdisciplinary care

Transdisciplinary care may still involve a number of people involved in your child's care, but this number tends to be reduced because the professionals work to some degree across professional boundaries. This model can work reasonably well with allied health professionals such as physios, OTs and speech pathologists, because the boundaries of the roles of these professions can be a little more fluid. For example, using a transdisciplinary approach, your child's physiotherapist might review your child's gross motor skills, but they might also review and address tasks such as dressing, handwriting or using cutlery that are typically managed by an OT (and vice versa – the OT can review and address your child's gross motor skills). This model can be useful for children who cope better with having fewer people involved in their care, and whose needs are less complex so could be covered by a smaller number of health professionals.

Key worker model of care

A key worker model involves a single health professional working with families in a guide role across different disciplines as well as different environments. Using this model, your child might be allocated a single key worker, who supports you and your child with all of their developmental needs across all areas and all environments. You may still have a number of other health professionals involved in your child's care; however, your child's key worker is your single first point of contact for all of your child's needs, and is your go-to person for information, resources and support. This model of care can be useful for children whose needs require coordination across different areas and environments, and also for families who will benefit from the direct support and coaching of the key worker.

Environmental enrichment

Environmental enrichment refers to an approach where the therapist helps you and your family set up stimulating activities and environments in your child's usual environments, such as at home and at day care, so that your child has lots of naturally occurring opportunities throughout the day to practise and develop their skills. For example, a therapist might set up an A-frame with lots of interesting toys or objects hanging from it to encourage your child to reach and grasp and finger the objects hanging from it. Your child's therapist might also set you up with some routines and activities to provide your child with numerous opportunities to practise new skills.

Environmental enrichment recognises that the more opportunities your child has to practise their skills, the more likely they are to consolidate and learn those skills. It also recognises the importance of child-led learning (see part IV for more on this), and that it is not always up to you, the parent, to facilitate your child's development. And even if you did, it is not possible for you to facilitate as much practice as what can be achieved by setting up your child's environment to be stimulating and facilitating of their developmental progress.

Parent coaching

Parent coaching is when a therapist teaches you, the parent, how to support and facilitate your child's development. The therapist might show you how to identify relevant situations, and then teach you to hold, move, choose activities, prompt and engage with your child. Parent coaching aims to empower you to be able to support your child throughout your and their everyday life. Parent coaching also recognises that, as a parent, you have the most influence on your child and have the most opportunity to support your child's development because you are with them more often and, therefore, have the biggest opportunity to influence the way they do things.

Direct hands-on therapy

This is where the therapist works directly with your child in a one-on-one situation to help teach, facilitate and support their development of specific skills. Direct hands-on therapy is ideal when your child is learning something new and requires direct help to learn the skill. Therapists are trained at monitoring and adapting activities and their handling from moment to moment, so this approach is great for the early learning stages of any new skill. Once your child has learnt the skill and can satisfactorily do the skill (even if it is not perfect yet), your child's therapist will challenge your child by making the skill harder or getting them to do the skill in a variety of different ways. Alternatively, the therapist will move onto the next skill. Once your child has learnt the skill, practise of that skill can then also occur at home and in your child's other environments to continue to consolidate and master the skill.

Regular review appointments

Regular appointments involve your child receiving, for example, fortnightly or monthly appointments with a therapist or teacher, and their progress being reviewed and advanced at each session. This approach is suitable for children who are progressing reasonably well with less-intensive supports, such as enhancing their environments, a little facilitation and coaching from the therapist, and home activities supported by their parents and family.

Intensive therapy

Intensive therapy is a way of scheduling a number of appointments over a short period of time. For example, your child might receive two sessions of therapy per day for one week, totalling 10 hours of therapy in a week. At our clinic, we use the intensive therapy approach for two reasons:

1. *To provide goal-directed therapy (when your child is working towards a specific skill):* Having appointments close together when working towards a specific goal allows your child to intensely practise new skills, and the repetition of practising these activities throughout the course of an intensive block allows your child to learn and retain the new skill. We often find that children can learn a new skill in an intensive block that would perhaps have otherwise taken them many weeks due to the less frequent practice that occurs when they receive therapy once a week or fortnight.

2. *To decrease or shift the demand on parents and families:* Many of the children we see at our clinic receive lots of therapy. They might be seeing three to four different therapists each week, each for a one hour session. This means parents have to be available to get their child to each session, which, over a period of time, can be very tiring for parents and children, especially if the children are school aged and attending school between 9 am and 3 pm as well! So, for some families, we will schedule them in for a block of therapy once a term, or in each school holiday, so that they receive the same dosage of therapy (for example, 10 hours) but over a shorter period of time (say, over one to two weeks instead of over 10 weeks).

In between blocks of therapy, families get to have a break from running their child to and from appointments, and get to just enjoy spending time together as a family (although we do recommend children continue with home exercise activities in between blocks of therapy to maintain the gains achieved).

Home programs

Home programs are frequently prescribed by therapists to help your child increase their amount of practice of certain activities or exercises in between therapy sessions or appointments. Ideally, the home program activities should be activities that have been practised within a therapy session, and your child repeats the activity as part of the home program. The program might recommend a number of practice sessions to be done per week, or alternatively it might recommend pairing an activity with another daily habit in an attempt to introduce repetition of an activity or to introduce a new beneficial habit. A way to increase your child's motivation to complete the home programs can be by using sticker or star charts, and creating weekly goals with small rewards at the end of the week.

Therapy assistants

Similar to home programs, therapy assistants are sometimes recommended to help increase the amount of home activities or exercises your child practises in between therapy appointments. The therapy assistant is like an extra set of hands for you to be able to complete a home program regularly, or to help keep your child motivated while completing the home program. By increasing the amount, repetition or dosage of home activities your child is doing (and based on the principles of neuroplasticity), the aim is to help your child to improve in their function more quickly.

Therapy assistants often cost less than therapists, so parents or funding agencies can sometimes push to use therapy assistants 'instead of' therapists. It is important to understand that a therapy assistant does not replace the need for a therapist. Therapy assistants do not have the same level of training a therapist does, which means they do not have the knowledge and clinical reasoning to be able to adapt an activity on the spot to make it easier or harder for your child like a therapist will. As a result, your child is unlikely to be able to be challenged to progress by a therapy assistant in the way a therapist will challenge them. Therapy assistants are great for consolidating skills that are newly learnt, or for increasing strength and endurance in activities, but these activities should always initially be done under the supervision of a qualified therapist who will make sure the activities are safe for your child to do, and that the therapy assistant is able to complete the activities with your child safely. The therapist will then also need to review your child's progress, and update the activities intermittently to ensure your child's optimal progression.

Therapy in natural environments versus clinic situations

Therapy and other supports can be delivered in clinics or in other natural environments such as your home, your child's day care or school, or the local playground, beach or pool. Either option (clinical or natural) has benefits, and the right option for you and your child will depend on your and your child's needs. Some children are more comfortable being seen at home, in their own environment.

Some children are highly distractible at home, and are better off being seen at a clinic. Some children enjoy getting to play with new toys when they come to the clinic. Some children have preferred toys at home and, therefore, participate in therapy better at home. Sometimes your child might be able to access specific equipment (like a suspension hoist over a treadmill to practise walking) only if you attend the clinic. Sometimes it is cheaper to see your child's therapist at the clinic because having them come out to home incurs an additional cost. You need to discuss with your child's therapist the options available to you, and which environments will best suit your child's needs.

Face to face versus virtual or telehealth care

Another less common, but quite useful, option you may wish to consider is receiving your child's therapy via 'telehealth'. Telehealth is a way of delivering a health or therapy service virtually, over the computer and usually via a video link. While telehealth used to only be available in hospitals and health services and required some fairly sophisticated (and expensive!) equipment, the improvements in internet services in Australia means telehealth is now quite readily available for people just using their home computers. Many research projects have shown that delivery of telehealth services can be just as good as having a face-to-face appointment with a doctor or therapist.

Telehealth can be a useful option if you cannot or would prefer not to access local services because:

- You live in a rural or remote area.
- Your child is medically fragile, does not cope in different environments and with different people, or is in a lot of pain, and leaving the house for appointments is difficult, fatiguing or disruptive.
- Your child needs access to specialist services, and that service is not available in your town or city.

Telehealth can also be a useful option if the approach to therapy for your child requires a parent-coaching approach. In that situation, you can do a telehealth appointment with the health professional who provides you with coaching and guidance on strategies that you then implement with your child.

How to decide which approach is right for your child and family

Deciding which care approach is right for your child and family can be quite a personal decision, but an important one to consider. The list of approaches I have covered in this chapter is not exhaustive – it simply provides you with a general overview and description of some of the common approaches used in early childhood intervention. Different service providers may adopt a single approach, or a combination of approaches. Your child might benefit from different approaches at different stages in their childhood, or for different situations. For example, some children might benefit from regular therapy reviews, but have that interspersed with periods of intensive therapy during significant developmental periods. Alternatively, some children might receive regular therapy from local providers, but then also receive care via telehealth for specialty services not available in their local town.

To decide which approach might be right for your child, work through the following:

- Talk with your child's therapist about how your child is progressing, and whether any approach is likely to help your child to progress faster or further.
- Consider how your child might cope with each different approach. Does your child cope better with higher or lower intensity intervention? Will they cope if more people are involved in your child's care? Do they respond better to others or to you?

- Consider your family circumstances, and what feels right for you as a parent and for your family.
- Consider what your needs are as a parent. Would you prefer to coordinate your child's care yourself, or would you prefer to have a key worker to assist with this? What approach do you feel will suit you personally as a parent, within the context of your own personality and life?
- Consider the time commitment that might be required of different approaches, and what will fit in with your child's and family's other commitments.
- Talk with other parents whose child is using a different approach. You could ask them how they are finding the alternative approach, and what they have found to be the pros and cons of the approach.

Remember, you can always use a combination of approaches; you don't have to pick only one option. And you can also change the approach you use if you find one is not working for you or your child or family, or if your child's or family's needs change. The most important thing to consider is if the approach feels right to you for your child and family.

Recognising your child's needs summary points

- All areas of your child's development are interconnected and have an impact on each other.

- Your child's essential health and wellbeing will always take precedence over their development. And if these essential needs are not being met, their development will take a 'back seat' to your child's survival.

- Your child's development will follow a continual process of learning and refining new skills, and their developmental progress will be affected by a multitude of things, including their personality, their condition, and the physical and social environment.

- Your child has strengths and talents that you can build upon and utilise to assist your child in developing their independence and self-identify.

- When deciding on goals or focus areas for your child to work towards improving, consider both urgent and important tasks, and think of what your child needs to be able to manage in the future, as well as the present.

- When starting out with therapies and services, try to find providers or services you trust, who help you to feel confident and empowered, and who feel like a good fit for your child and family.

Part III: Assist, but don't insist

Rowan is a ten-year-old boy with an unknown congenital condition causing physical, communication and cognitive difficulties. He can sit up without help, but cannot move about the floor, stand up without help or the use of a standing frame, and he cannot walk without the use of a walker. He has limited use of his hands – he can reach and swipe or bat at things with his hands, and can open his hands to grasp things, but he generally does not use his hands for play or function. He is unable to communicate using his voice or his hands, although he does make eye contact. Rowan has a very severe disability, and requires assistance with every aspect of his life. How can we help Rowan to be independent, when he is so physically and cognitively dependent on his parents and other people for every aspect of his life? What does independence look like for a child like Rowan?

Not all children have as many difficulties as Rowan. However, all children with developmental delays and disabilities will have some level of difficulties for which they will need help. So how can we make sure we find a balance between giving them the help they need and also supporting them to become as independent as possible?

If you search the dictionary for the word independent, the following definitions come up:

1. Not influenced or controlled by others in matters of opinion, conduct, etc.; thinking or acting for oneself

2. Not subject to another's authority or jurisdiction; autonomous; free
3. Not influenced by the thought or action of others
4. Not dependent; not depending or contingent upon something else for existence, operation, etc.

Each of these definitions reflects a sense of autonomy, self-direction, self-reliance or of being separate from others. While children, by nature, regardless of their abilities or disabilities, have some degree of dependence on us as their parents, our role is to gradually teach them to become more independent, not just physically but also with their choices, decisions and level of responsibility.

While your child with a developmental delay or disability will require more assistance from you or other people than a child who does not have a developmental delay or disability, it is important that we "assist, but don't insist", in order to help them to become as independent as possible. 'Assisting, but not insisting' is a phrase I have developed that aims to describe this balance between the need to support and assist your child in their everyday life, but also the need to let go and give them opportunity to do things for themselves and become independent, self-directed and self-driven adults, as much as they possibly can be.

In the chapters in this part, we will explore how it is you can help your child to become as independent as possible, within the context of their developmental delay or disability. Two key approaches can be used to help your child to develop their independence, both physically and mentally. One is a rehabilitative approach – that is, we utilise and improve your child's own abilities and competencies to promote independence – while the second is more of an accommodative and adaptive approach, in which we can use equipment, technologies and supports to assist your child to become as independent as possible. Many children end up using a combination of these approaches in order to become as independent as possible, and both these approaches are covered in the following chapters.

CHAPTER TEN

Looking at what's important

For most children with developmental delays or disabilities, some degree of improvement is possible, both physically and mentally. Neuroplasticity, as discussed in chapter 1, allows for these improvements to occur. The amount of 'organic' improvement possible will vary depending on your child's condition and the natural potential for improvement. Importantly, the way your child is supported to improve their developmental skills can play a big role in their overall development of independence.

This chapter aims to help you to understand the important foundational concepts or strategies that will help you to support your child to build their independence throughout their rehabilitation or therapy journey. Certain methods to support your child are important to giving them opportunity to develop their physical independence and their self-determination. By understanding these concepts and strategies, you will be providing your child with the best opportunity to become as independent as possible.

Choice-making and self-initiated movement, activity and communication

Your child might not be as physically or cognitively dependent or disabled as Rowan (introduced at the beginning of this part). However, regardless of whether your child has a developmental delay or disability or not, the ability to make a choice is the first stage of your child developing their independence.

The earliest form of choice-making seen in babies and children is their ability to initiate movement for a purpose – that is, they choose to move for some reason. For example, when your child is learning to swipe at a toy, they are motivated by the toy, and they are choosing to initiate that movement in an attempt to reach or touch the toy. When your child learns to roll to get to a favourite toy, they are initiating that movement, because they are choosing which toy they want to play with. When they move from one place in a room to another, whether that be by rolling, crawling, walking or driving a power wheelchair, they are making a choice about where they want to be in their environment.

The ability to make choices enables your child to develop their sense of independence, and means your child has a say in what happens to them. Through making choices, your child is learning to recognise they are separate from you and are their own person, who can decide things for themselves.

To make a choice, whether it is to move, to make a sound or play with a toy, your child needs to:

- recognise that they have an option in order to be able to make a choice
- be motivated to make a choice
- be able to initiate a response in order to make that choice.

Supporting your child in their learning about choice making may involve the following:

- *Not doing everything for your child:* Instead, allow your child opportunity to do things and explore for themselves. Follow your child's lead. (See part IV for more on this.)
- *Giving them freedom for movement and exploration:* Support your child to learn to move by themselves, and provide an environment that is stimulating so that they are motivated to explore through their own self-initiated reaching, touching, banging, rolling, crawling or walking.
- *Giving them options to be able to make a choice:* For most children, this starts with a very simple choice of stopping or starting an activity or requesting more of a favourite activity. And your child does not need to be able to give a verbal response in order to make a choice and request more. Your child can indicate a request for more by vocalising, via a physical response such as tapping, scratching or banging, or by using their eyes.
- *Waiting patiently for them to give a response to show they have made a choice:* Some children have much slower processing times than what we, as adults, are used to. If you have ever asked a four year old which ice-cream flavour they would like, you would know that children can take longer to make a choice than adults. And if your child has a developmental delay or disability, they might have slower processing time, which will mean it will take longer to make a choice. Give your child time to process what the options are, and time to then make a decision.
- *Expect and accept that your child will make mistakes when making choices:* Making decisions, and specifically making good decisions, is a learnt skill.

The importance of play and self-initiated activity

As Fred Rogers, American writer, producer and creator of the preschool television series *Mister Rogers' Neighborhood*, argued, 'Play is often talked about as if it were a relief from serious learning. But for children, play is serious learning. Play is really the work of childhood.' This idea carries across to your child's therapy. When your child is attending therapy sessions, it might look like your child is just playing. This is a common comment (or complaint) I see on online forums from parents, and I can understand why. As therapists, we sometimes don't explain the intricacies of what we are working on with your child during the therapy session. We might explain it at the beginning or the end of the session, but during the session we are focused on engaging your child in participating in the activities we have set out for them.

Playing, however, is an essential requirement to helping your child learn to self-initiate movements and activities, to make choices, and to problem-solve – all essential components of learning about themselves and the world around them, and all skills that underpin your child's ability to develop independence. Engaging your child in play is the best way to ensure your child is self-initiating movement, activities and interactions, rather than us just telling them what to do or making them do something. Engaging your child through play is how your child learns that they have choices within the activities and can contribute to the outcomes of the activities. Engaging in play, initiating movement and actions, and making choices, is how your child learns and lays down new pathways in their brains. While the play activity might start off by showing and guiding your child on how to do the activity, the ultimate goal is for your child to be able to take over and do that activity for themselves. To be able to do this, your child needs to be able to engage in the activity, recognise that they have a role in making choices within that activity, and initiate the movements and actions to carry out the activity. Without this self-initiated movement, your child is just a passive participant in the therapy, and the carry over into everyday real life will not be realised.

I cannot stress enough to you how important self-initiated activity is for your child. I am disappointed to say I have seen a number of children who have attended treatment programs that simply apply a treatment *to* a child, instead of having the child participate actively and engage in choice-making as part of the therapy process. And the difference in outcomes for these children in terms of independence is vast.

Case studies

Imagine two children, Kate and Robert, with identical disabilities. Both children are the same age, with the same abilities and difficulties, and the same advantages in life. Both children are working towards learning to crawl and stand, and are attending an intensive therapy program. The therapy programs they attend are exactly the same in terms of the amount of therapy provided, the intensity of therapy provided and the skill of the clinician. The only difference between the two experiences is the level of engagement and self-initiated activity that is provided within the treatment program. This can now be imagined as a kind of 'sliding doors' example of how different the outcome can be.

Kate attends a therapy program that pushes her to do as much as she physically can, by applying physical supports and taking Kate through specific movements such as crawling actions or standing up. Kate's therapist holds her in place, and facilitates all the movements she does. However, most of the therapy during this therapy block is done *to* Kate, not *with* Kate. Kate does not initiate the activities and she has little engagement with the activities. This approach will definitely help Kate experience what it feels like to crawl and stand, help Kate lay down sensory pathways in her brain, and will potentially improve her positioning and strength in the positions she is being held in. However, Kate's involvement in the therapy is rather passive, and because everything done to Kate is so passive, she has no sense of control or contribution to the therapy she is receiving.

In her therapy, Kate is not given a reason to move, and so does not learn through this process that moving has a point and a reason behind it. So even if during therapy Kate can be facilitated by her therapist to crawl, and even if she manages to do this without too much support from the therapist, until Kate realises the reason behind why she is crawling (that is, to get from one place to another), then she is still never going to choose to crawl in her everyday life.

In comparison, Robert attends a therapy program that adopts a play-based, child-led approach that engages and requires active initiation and participation of the child in the therapy. Similar to the therapy attended by Kate, during his therapy sessions Robert is supported and facilitated by the therapist to help learn patterns of movement. However, the focus of each treatment activity is on Robert interacting with the toys, environment or people in the room, and on learning to self-initiate the movement for a purpose – all of which is achieved through play. The therapist follows Robert's lead, and supports his attempts at movements to help him complete the movements and activities he initiates. The focus of Robert's therapy sessions is on Robert learning to initiate and control his movements for a purpose, something that he is motivated for. In comparison to Kate, Robert will learn reasons *why* he might choose to crawl or stand – for example, because it helps him to get to the toys he likes, he can explore the room or he can get closer to Mum for a song. As a result of understanding the purpose for crawling or standing, Robert is more likely to then replicate the movements he has learnt in therapy spontaneously in his everyday life.

Intentional movement and learning new skills

Learning to intentionally move their body for a purpose – whether it be to move from one place to another, to explore what is around them, access a switch, or to interact with others, and through

Looking at what's important

self-initiated and purposeful play – is so important to your child then being able to learn other skills that can help them to become more independent. For example, learning to move from one place to another, regardless of whether your child achieves this by rolling, creeping on their tummy, crawling, walking or driving themselves in a power wheelchair, has very far-reaching impacts on so many other aspects of your child's development. Regardless of the method of movement, the benefit comes from being able to *choose* to move.

Being able to move intentionally for a purpose provides the following benefits for your child:

- *Your child will have the opportunity to make a choice:* Your child will be able to choose to move, or choose to stay where they are. They will be able to choose to move to one place, but not to another. Or they might choose to touch the new toy, or choose not to. The simple act of initiating and moving is a choice that your child is able to make.

- *Your child will learn that they are a separate person to you, and that they have the opportunity to be independent:* They will learn that they are not dependent on you for their every need by the simple act of being able to choose to move from one place to another, or choosing to explore their environment with their hands without your help.

- *Your child will have the opportunity to explore, which will support their learning and understanding of the world:* By moving from one place to another, or exploring different parts of their environment, your child will gain a new perspective on the world. They will see, feel, hear, touch, taste and smell things from a different perspective. This can help their learning by comparing these new experiences with what they already know.

- *Your child will have the opportunity to problem-solve:* If, after moving, your child gets stuck, they will have the opportunity to try to problem-solve their way out of that. Even if their solution is to cry out to let you know they are stuck, they have still been able to recognise that they are stuck, that they need help, and that they had to vocalise to get some help. If your child reaches out for a toy but didn't find the toy they wanted or expected, they again have the opportunity to problem-solve how to get what they actually wanted, or to refine their attempt at moving for the next time.

Case study

Children with significant multiple impairments including cortical visual impairments are very dependent on others for their movement and everyday care. These children are often initially not able to communicate their wants or needs, or have limited ability to do so. In addition, these children can initially find it difficult to engage in play during therapy. Think about this from the child's perspective – they cannot see what is around them or move in order to go to what they want or get away from something, and are essentially at the mercy of the people in their lives, including their therapists. As a result, it can be very difficult to engage these children in active self-initiated play. However, I want to stress how important it is to actually engage these children in play during therapy, and not just push them through therapy without their active participation – for example, by actively engaging them in simple play such as exploring objects and textures with their fingers and hands, and contribution to initiating some of the movements. They likely need longer to recognise and respond to stimulus, but this response is still possible and should be waited for.

The key part of learning new skills and independence with new skills is in the child's ability to *self-initiate* the movement and activity. This involves your child independently choosing to move themselves for a specific purpose, regardless of what that movement is. As long as your child is independently choosing to initiate the movement and is actively engaging in the activity, the benefits listed in this section can be achieved.

The importance of alignment and posture

Theoretically, a healthy well-functioning human body is built to move efficiently and effectively – that is, to move easily and successfully, and with the least amount of effort or energy possible. This occurs due to the optimal alignment of our body parts, and optimal muscle activation in both an optimal pattern and to an optimal force. For children with disabilities, the optimal alignment, recruitment of muscles and activation of muscles can be disrupted. As a result, children with disabilities do not always move with optimal efficiencies.

Elite athletes train repetitively to hone their performance of a specific skill in terms of speed, accuracy, or efficiency. They have a coach (or a number of coaches) who provide constant or regular feedback on the performance of their specific skills. Their coaches will provide feedback on their body postures, body alignments, muscle activations, techniques, and performance. The athlete then uses all this feedback to improve their performance.

Children with a disability want the same outcomes as elite athletes – they want their body to be able to perform at their best, so that they can be the best they can be. To have their body perform at their best, they need optimal alignment, muscle activation, force production, and patterns of movement for efficient and effective skills. Both groups, elite athletes and people with a disability, want to improve their performance and maximise what their body can do for them – so essentially, our approach to doing this should be the same.

Some ways you and your therapist can be ensuring optimal alignment and posture for your child when performing tasks include:

- *Starting in an optimal position:* This might mean your child sitting in an optimal position before standing up or while practising writing with their hands.

- *Supporting your child's body to remain in an optimal position while they are practising a task:* This can be done by using your hands (or the therapist using their hands) to support your child's body alignment during a task. You or your child's therapist can also use supportive braces or garments such as orthotics, Theratogs or supportive equipment to maintain an optimal alignment (see the next chapter for more on this).

- *Making sure the choice of activity is not too difficult for your child:* If the activity is too difficult, your child is more likely to use compensatory patterns of movement or compensatory strategies, which if practised frequently enough can become habitual.

- *Provide constructive feedback to your child on their performance, at a level they will understand:* This allows them to make adjustments to improve their performance.

- *Practise intensely:* Elite athletes practise their sports intensely in an effort to become the best they can be at those particular skills. And elite performers such as singers and dancers practise their crafts intensely. Professionals also practise intensely – for example, surgeons will practise their surgery skills – in order to perfect their abilities. If your child can practise as intensely as these elite athletes, performers or professionals do, you can expect their abilities and skills to improve as well. Which brings me to the next point …

The importance of repetition

Have you ever seen a baby do the same movement over and over and over again? Have you ever wondered why they do that? I remember when my son had just learnt to pull up to standing. He could get himself to upright at the little play kitchen we have, and he was pretty proud of himself. The problem was he didn't know how to get back down again. So he would stand up, be super excited for a minute or so, and then cry pretty loudly because he was stuck and did not know what to do to get down again. So I would dutifully go over to him, help him by showing him how he could bend his legs to get his bottom onto the ground, and then go back to the job I was doing (which more often than not seemed to be cooking dinner). But guess

Looking at what's important

what he would do then? Yep – stand right on back up again! Again, he would stand there proudly and excitedly until he realised he was stuck, and then would cry loudly again until I came back over to rescue him from this new skill of standing up. This constant repetition of standing up and crying until someone saved him meant that it took me soooo much longer to cook dinner than it probably should have. But it also was a fantastic example of how children repeatedly practise tasks over and over again to refine their skills.

Repetition is how your child will master learning movements and skills. Just as an elite athlete trains repetitively, practising and mastering their skills over and over again to improve their performance, your child also needs to repeatedly practise their skills to enable them to get better and better at the skill, movement or activity.

So what is it about that repetition that allows your child to continually improve their performance?

This is related to the feedback–feedforward loop. Any time your child attempts or practises a skill, they experience feedback from the environment and their body about how successfully they were able to complete that task. For example, if your child is learning to pick up a small toy, when they first try to reach for the toy, they might touch it with their hand but are unable to grasp it. During that first attempt, your child will have felt their arm reaching for the toy, seen and felt the direction of the reach, seen and felt their hand touching the toy, felt their hand closing but no toy being in their hand. They then might look at their hand, turn their hand up to see that the toy is not in their hand (which reinforces what they felt – that there was no toy in their hand), and then look back at the toy to reinforce that the toy is still where it was, and not in their hand where they wanted it to be. All of this sensory information is providing feedback to your child to understand their performance of the task and how it affected the outcome.

On the second attempt, your child might have a more direct reach for the toy, and they may pause for longer with their hand over the toy to allow them to close their fingers around it to grasp it. They will then feel the toy in their hand, turn their hand to look at the toy (which reinforces what they are feeling in their hand), and look back at where the toy was to confirm that their attempt at reach and grasp was successful. Now maybe your child wants to put that toy in their mouth, but the way they have grasped it means that they cannot get it into their mouth. The feedback your child receives through their eyes, their hands, their mouth, their arms and their environment will provide them with further feedback to refine their reach and grasp the next time to make sure that the toy is grasped more with their thumb and first two fingers, rather than with their little fingers (which will make it easier to get the toy to their mouth).

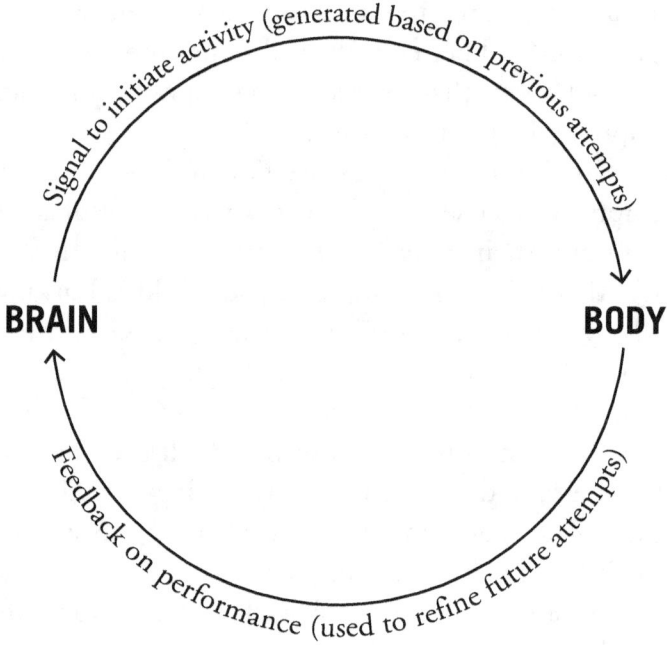

This process of feedback and feedforward constantly provides your child with information to refine their performance of all skills. When a child is learning to make sounds in preparation for speech, hold and use a pencil or use their vision to focus and make a choice through eye contact, they are constantly receiving feedback about their performance of that task, which they can use to improve their future performance. Repetitively training your child's body to perform a task will help them to refine the pathways in their brain at a neurological level, which will enhance their efficiency and effectiveness in the future.

Repetition is particularly important for your child with a disability for two reasons:

1. *Children with physical disabilities often don't get opportunity for repetition:* Children with physical disabilities may have decreased ability to move, to interact, or to explore their environment which means they have less opportunity to practise and improve their skills. Typically developing children practise their skills hundreds and thousands of times a day. In comparison, when learning new skills, children with physical disabilities might practise their movement skills 50 to 100 times during a therapy session and another 50 to 100 times per day when Mum or Dad or other family members help them to practise at home during the week. That is a vastly different number of opportunities for practice, and so a vastly different number of opportunities for your child to master their skills.

2. *Children with cognitive disabilities or learning difficulties require more practice:* Children with difficulties in their thinking skills have more trouble retaining and recalling information. So when they practise a new skill, they may not as easily recall previous unsuccessful attempts that would otherwise help them to improve their performance in the future. As a result, in order to learn a new movement, skill or strategy, a child with a disability may require more practice in order to retain that skill and then also use it spontaneously in their everyday life.

How can you increase repetition of practice for your child?

Here are some tips to help your child increase repetition of their practice:

- Talk to your child's therapist about your child's progress and whether you think increasing the repetition of practice of a specific skill would be helpful. Your child's therapist might be able to narrow down the different types of activities done within a session so more repetition of a single activity can occur, or provide you with more strategies you can practise with your child at home.

- Recruit the help of other people to help your child practise. This might be your child's teachers, their grandparents, their siblings, or even neighbours and friends. Alternatively, you could look at finding a therapy assistant who could help your child to practise between therapy sessions.

- Build the activity you child needs to practise into their daily routine. Maybe you can practise the activity every time your child goes to the toilet, or after every mealtime. Maybe your child can practise the activity on the drive to school each morning. Building the practice of an activity into your child's daily routine will help to decrease the feeling of trying to fit even more into your child's busy day.

- Find ways to set up your child within their environments (at home, at kindy or school) so that they can practise the skills independently. (This approach is called environmental enrichment and is introduced in the previous chapter.) Enriching your child's environments with spaces and opportunities for them to initiate and practise an activity means they can practise it repeatedly throughout their day without (or with less prompting from) you.

- Find community activities, such as specific sports, play groups and music groups, which will assist your child in practising the skill throughout the week.

- If feasible, consider increasing the number of therapy sessions or the length of therapy sessions your child does (funding limits may make this difficult, plus you still want to make sure you keep a balance between therapy and free play).

The importance of variety

Variety is the spice of life, as they say. In the case of opportunities to practise skills and abilities, variety of opportunities and situations is what enables us to adapt our skills to the various tasks required in our lives. For example, reaching above your head can be used for pushing your arm through a sleeve, pegging clothes up on the line, putting a cup away in the cupboard, washing or brushing your hair.

It is important for your child to develop a wide variety of abilities, and to be able to apply their abilities in a wide variety of situations. Your child's abilities in each developmental area can be described as a 'repertoire' – a stock of skills or types of behaviours that your child typically uses. The wider your child's repertoire of skills, the more ability and therefore independence they will have, across many different environments. What this means is that your child will be able to adapt their movement, communication or self-care abilities to the very many tasks, environments or situations they might have to manage in their lives. Developing a wide foundation of skills, or a wide repertoire of skills, allows your child to problem-solve and develop independence, through being able to adapt their skills to a variety of situations.

Typically, children with disabilities lack a variety of movements or a variety of communication and self-care skills, due to both neurological and developmental issues, or due to the development of habitual patterns. This is particularly apparent in the development of movement skills. As already discussed earlier in this book, once your child learns to move using one pattern, if they don't have the opportunity to adapt that movement skill through practising a variety of movements and in different positions, activities and environments, they will not learn to move in any other way. This lack of movement repertoire in children with disabilities can be likened to a builder only having a hammer with which to build a house. Children with disabilities without a wide movement repertoire use their 'hammer' to achieve all of their movement tasks. In all fairness, when building a house you can probably use a hammer to break up long pieces of wood, stir the concrete, and try to make sure the walls are level to the ground – but the end result could be very messy or largely unsuccessful. Or the desired outcome may have been achieved, but only through a great deal more effort. The same goes for your child with a disability who is moving using only one strategy. Their movements will be effortful, messy, inefficient, and sometimes unsuccessful. It is our aim, as therapists and parents, to help your child to learn new ways of moving, communicating, and thinking, so that your child can learn to cope in a variety of situations and environments. You and your child's therapy team will do this by teaching your child new patterns of movement, new ways to do or learn an activity or task, and to think about problems or themselves, their feelings or emotions in a new way. You can also do this by layering new skills on top of old skills, and extending upon your child's skills to expand their skill repertoire.

How can you increase variety of practice for your child?

To help your child increase variety in their practice, try the following:

- Slightly (or greatly) adjust the set-up of the environment in which your child is practising a skill. This might be by slightly changing the toy position to encourage your child to, for example, reach differently or move differently. Or it could be using slightly different toys or objects – for example, using a different sized pencil or a different style of keypad.
- Practise the skills in a variety of environments, including familiar environments, unfamiliar environments, quiet and busy environments, and inside and outside.
- Ask your child a question or prompt your child in a slightly different way. This will help them to think differently about the question or direction you have given them.
- Prompt your child to extend upon skills they have already mastered. For example, if your child has already mastered how to request their favourite toy using the communication book, you could ask them, demonstrate for them, or teach them to request a different toy, or to say something different about their favourite toy.

The importance of interaction and communication

The key to independence for children with disabilities – including those with severe disabilities – is in their ability to make choices and then to communicate their wants and needs. It is in your child's ability to communicate 'yes' or 'no' about what happens to them and their body in their lives. It doesn't matter if this 'yes' or 'no' is communicated by nodding or shaking their head, by pressing a switch, or by vocalising the words. The ability to choose a response, and have that response respected by whomever they are talking to, is an enormous opportunity for independence for children with disabilities who have significant physical or communication difficulties.

In order to be able to make choices and communicate their wants and needs, your child first needs to:

- feel safe, comfortable, calm and regulated
- have the ability to remain engaged during an interaction with another person
- understand that they have something to say, and that other people will listen to them
- have a motor or cognitive strategy of some sort that they can use to get their message across (whether that strategy is oral, by pointing or gesturing, or using a switch to activate a communication device).

As you can see, the ability to communicate is underpinned by a lot more than just being able to get a message across to another person. And for children with autism, some genetic conditions and complex neurological disabilities, their ability to communicate can be impeded by their physical, sensory or cognitive difficulties. It is important to explore what difficulties your child is experiencing that are affecting their abilities to communicate, and make sure these are addressed as best as possible.

Repetition of practice is also as important to learning to communicate as it is to learning any other skill. Typically developing babies spend the first 12 months of their life listening to the people around them talk before they say their first word. It is important to keep this 12-month time frame in mind when your child is first learning to communicate using an alternative strategy such as signing or a communication book. Your child might require hundreds of practice attempts, through watching you and practising with you, before they independently initiate communication themselves.

How can you increase opportunities for your child to learn and practise communicating?

Here are some examples of how you can provide opportunity for interaction and communication practice in your child's everyday life:

- Learn to use their communication strategy yourself, and model using the communication strategy as you talk to your child.

- Teach other people involved in your child's care to also use the same communication strategy with your child. Consistency in the way people communicate with your child provides the repetition they need to learn.

- Make sure your child's communication strategy is always accessible to them. If your child is using picture communication, make sure they can see and reach their communication board or book. If your child is using a switch and or an electronic device, make sure it is always within their reach. And make sure your child's communication device goes everywhere with your child so that they can consistently use it in all environments (or adapt the communication device to the environment – for example, I have seen communication boards laminated and stuck down onto kickboards for children to use during swimming lessons).

- Give your child time to process, understand and respond. When interacting with your child, make sure you pause and wait for their response. Some children may need additional time to understand what has been said to them, may just be learning about taking turns when communicating, or may need additional time to think about what or how they want to respond and also to initiate and complete the communication attempt.

- Build practising communication into their play and everyday activities. Some ideas for this include:
    - comment on things you or your child are doing
    - ask your child questions, and give them opportunity to answer (or you can model an answer if your child is not up to that stage yet)
    - express how you are feeling or how your child is feeling
    - give your child opportunities to make choices – offer them a choice of two toys, or a choice between two different options for lunch.
- Always respond to your child's attempts to communicate, even if you are not sure what they are saying, or you think it looks like they are playing – remember that even typically developing children start by babbling and making sounds that don't actually mean anything, but by responding positively to their attempts at communication, and helping them to practise turn-taking and sounds, they gradually improve their communication skills over time.

CHAPTER ELEVEN

Assistive technology and equipment

When your child is still young or if they're only newly diagnosed, it can take some time for you as a parent to be 'ready' to accept your child needing some assistive technology, particularly a wheelchair or power wheelchair, or an electronic communication device. Perhaps you are worried that adopting a piece of assistive technology early will prevent your child from learning to achieve the overall goal you would like for them– that is, walking and/or talking. Perhaps acceptance of the technology also involves final acceptance that your child's disability might stop them from ever achieving that overall goal of walking and talking, or affect them socially. However, introducing and helping your child use assistive technology can also provide some pretty significant benefits as well. In this chapter, I explore reasons accepting assistive technology might be difficult and help you to allay your fears. I then run through the huge variety of specialist equipment available and what it is for, to help you understand what might be beneficial for your child.

Accepting specialist equipment as needed

Using specialist adaptive equipment or technology does not prevent your child from being able to develop the ability to do a particular skill or activity later by themselves. If this is your worry, you are not alone – parents often worry that introducing a specific piece of equipment will hold their child back from eventually learning to do things independently, or 'normally'. For example, common concerns I have heard from parents are:

- 'I don't really want to get my child a wheelchair, because then he will get lazy and will always want to use the wheelchair, and won't walk/will lose his ability to walk.'
- 'I don't really want my child to learn to communicate with an iPad, because then she won't learn to talk.'
- 'I don't really want my child to learn to use a computer so early, because then she will never learn to write properly.'

When we break down these concerns, I often come up with two main underlying issues that parents have about introducing assistive technology or equipment for their child. The following sections address each of these issues in a little more detail, so you can understand these thought biases and can consider the introduction of adaptive equipment and technology in a more positive light.

Potential loss of skills or progress

Parents can sometimes be concerned that, as a result of introducing specialist equipment or technology, their child:

- might not develop as much as they otherwise could if they did not get the equipment or technology (for example, they will not learn to walk or talk, as a result of using adaptive equipment)
- might lose some skills as a result of choosing to use the assistive equipment (for example, losing walking skills or talking skills).

However, this kind of thinking ignores the potential gains to be made from the introduction of the equipment or technology, particularly from the point of the child becoming independent in their everyday life, and being able to participate in their everyday life. As discussed in part II, when considering your child's needs, it is important to understand their needs from a participation level, as well as an activity level. Adaptive equipment and technology will support your child's ability to do activities and participate in activities more successfully and independently in everyday life. The following two examples of a wheelchair and an electronic communication device illustrate how the introduction of each of these specialist equipment supports a child's participation.

Case study: Wheelchair and communication device

Wheelchairs are often recommended for either children who cannot walk, or children who can walk, but walking is effortful, painful or tiring. For the first set of children, the introduction of a wheelchair is reasonably obvious, because they need it every day for all of their mobility. In contrast, for the second set of children, sometimes the use of the wheelchair is recommended for in specific situations, such as when covering longer distances, over rough terrain where they are more likely to fall over, or in large crowds. The purpose of the wheelchair is to enhance that child's participation at school and in the community. Consider what could happen if the child was not provided with a wheelchair for those specific situations: The child would get tired, experience pain, or fall more frequently. If the child gets tired from just walking – for example, at school – this will affect their ability to participate in all other aspects of school. They might not be able to go to the library, because it is too far to walk. They might get so tired from just walking to the bathroom and back that they then cannot concentrate in the classroom, which will affect their learning. They might not be able to go on excursions with their peers, because they cannot keep up. Once a child is in high school and has to walk between every class, they might not be able to get to classes on time. In the community, if the child does not have a wheelchair, they may not be able to go out to socialise or attend and participate in events or activities because they might not be able to walk the longer distances, or they might not have the balance to be able to walk on uneven ground or in busy environments. The introduction of the wheelchair is aimed to assist the child to be able to manage the physical demands of their everyday life so that their social participation and learning is not compromised.

In the case of a communication device, it might be introduced because the child cannot speak or sign at all, so the communication device is their sole way to be able to communicate. Or it might be introduced because, even though the child can speak, their speech is not easily understood, or it is very quiet, slow or effortful. For the children in this category, their unclear, slow or effortful speech will affect their ability to communicate with others, because the people they are communicating with might not be able to understand what they are saying, or might not have the patience to wait for their full message to be said. (For example, if the child wanted to purchase a train ticket in a busy train station with a line of people behind them, it would be hard for them to get their message across to the ticket officer, and this would affect their ability to then catch the train.) Not being able to be understood by others is also highly frustrating for a child (or adult for that matter!), which can cause difficulties with behaviour and social interactions. The introduction of the communication device enhances the child's interaction and participation, helping them to more easily communicate with their parents, their siblings, their friends, and with other people including strangers in the community.

Assistive technology and equipment

I want to assure you that no therapist is going to prescribe a piece of equipment that your child does not need or will not benefit from. The trials and paperwork to apply for pieces of equipment are too onerous to go through unless it is actually necessary. In addition, funding agencies are definitely not going to fund something that they don't deem necessary. So if your child's therapist discusses the idea of using a wheelchair or a power wheelchair or a communication device, they are doing so because they think the device will help your child to progress their development. And if your child has access to these types of devices early in their life, they can develop some foundational understandings and abilities that will help them in their future development.

If your child learns to drive a power wheelchair early, this teaches them that they have capacity to move themselves wherever they would like within their environment, that they can explore their environment and the people and the things in it, and that they can make choices about where they want to be and who they want to spend time with. Additionally, your child will develop an understanding of depth perception, of cause and effect, and that they are a person separate to other people. All of this helps to develop their sense of self and independence.

Many a time I have overheard parents talking to each other about 'the speech therapist was teaching them to use the iPad to talk – that's not teaching them to talk, that's just teaching them to use the iPad!' However, this is not so simple. Communication is about sending a message to a communication partner and being understood, as well as understanding the messages coming to us from our communication partner. Being able to communicate enables your child to be heard. Without this, your child can experience frustration, which for most children can be seen as behavioural difficulties. The introduction of a communication device will not prevent your child from learning to talk – it just gives them an alternative form of communication to use to interact with others, until (if this eventuates for your child) they can talk to communicate instead. However, if your child has no way of communicating, and is given no alternative way of communicating, your child has no way of being heard or understood. Over a number of years of not being able to be heard or understood, your child will give up on trying to communicate, and may learn to not communicate at all. As you can hopefully see, your child is better off learning to communicate using an alternative method, rather than not at all.

In both the examples discussed in the case study, the introduction of the specialist equipment would not spell the end of your child's therapy journey towards learning to walk or talk. Your child's therapist will continue to work with your child on their ability to walk, either with aids or on their own, and their ability to talk using their own voice or by signing. And some children will, in fact, 'grow out' of the need to use a wheelchair or a communication device. However, the introduction of this specialist equipment at an appropriately early age means that your child does not miss out on the opportunity to improve their development in other areas, particularly their social participation and learning.

Acceptance of disability

The second underlying concern parents hold about introducing specialist equipment early is based on the negative connotations associated with disability equipment. Sometimes this concern is not immediately recognised by parents, and is instead an unconscious thought underlying their fear or resistance to the introduction of equipment or technology. Parents can be concerned that the introduction of disability-specific equipment will make their child look different, or look disabled. For example, a child using a wheelchair is immediately recognisable as having a disability – whereas a child in a specialised stroller 'looks less disabled'. Introducing a piece of disability-specific equipment requires you to accept that your child has a disability, and that your child will be readily recognised by others as having a disability.

It is easy to understand why this is a concern for parents. Unfortunately, not everyone in our society can recognise the capabilities of people with disability. As a parent, you don't want other people to automatically assume your child's capability, purely based upon the fact they use a wheelchair. You also don't want your child to be left out, teased or ignored, just because they are in a wheelchair or use a communication device. However, this is the 'catch 22' – without the introduction of the wheelchair or the communication device, your child won't be able to prove their capabilities to others anyway. If your child has no effective way to communicate with others, they won't be able to demonstrate how smart and capable they are. If your child has no effective and efficient way to move around in their world, they will miss out on opportunities to develop their capabilities in other areas and to interact and participate with others. So, it is important to remember that embracing this assistive equipment and technology can assist your child to develop their abilities, which will help them to become as independent as possible and to prove to other people and the world just how capable they really are.

Using the specialist equipment your child needs

A variety of specialised equipment is available to support your child's independence with their mobility and their daily life. This section provides a selection of common aids and equipment that we commonly recommend or trial in our clinic. This list is not exhaustive, and other items might be available for your child, so it is important to discuss your child's needs and goals with their therapists to come up with the best solutions for your child.

Orthoses and shoes

An orthosis (or orthoses in plural form) is any kind of brace or device worn on the outside of the body that aims to support the posture, alignment or function of that body part. For example, if your child's foot and ankle is well supported, your child has more opportunity to learn to control the movements of their knee, hip and trunk above. This can help them to stand and walk with better alignment and control. A well-supported spine can help to prevent your child from developing a scoliosis (curved spine). Most orthoses are named after the body part that they are supporting (for example, an ankle foot orthosis (AFO) supports the ankle and the foot).

Lower limb orthoses

Lower limb orthoses include AFOs, supramalleolar orthoses (SMOs), and knee-ankle-foot orthoses (KAFOs).

As suggested, lower limb orthoses are splints or braces applied to the foot and/or legs. These types of orthoses are designed to support the body part they are applied to (for example, a foot orthosis will support the bones and ligaments of your foot, an ankle foot orthosis will support both the ankle and the foot). By wearing a lower limb orthosis, the position and alignment of your child's foot and ankle is optimised, which can prevent them from developing contractures or deformities, and can allow for your child to have better control of the joints and muscles. Usually, foot and leg orthoses are prescribed to support your child's alignment and movements when they are sitting, standing and walking, so they are often worn during the day. However, sometimes a foot or leg orthosis is recommended to be worn only at night to try to prevent your child from developing contractures or deformities of their feet.

Sometimes a specific type of shoe or a shoe adaptation is recommended. Sometimes these shoes can be recommended instead of an orthosis, or they are recommended to be worn with an orthosis to assist with supporting the alignment of the foot and leg.

Body or trunk orthoses

As the name suggests, body or trunk orthoses – or thoracolumbosacral orthoses (TLSOs) – are splints or supports that are worn to support the trunk position. Two types of trunk orthoses are available – soft body orthosis or hard orthoses. Soft orthoses are usually made out of material, which usually has some stretch, and may or may not have extra strapping or solid stays (hard bands of plastic) to support your child's body alignment and posture. Examples of soft body orthoses include SPIO Vests, Theratogs, DMO Orthoses, and Second Skin orthoses. Soft orthoses are usually recommended to support not only your child's alignment and posture, but also, and importantly, their functional abilities. For example, if your child has difficulty activating their core trunk muscles, which is affecting their sitting posture and their ability to use their hands in a sitting position, your child's therapist might recommend that your child use a soft body orthosis to support their trunk alignment and control.

In comparison, hard body orthoses are usually recommended or prescribed by an orthopaedic doctor to try to prevent the deterioration of a child's scoliosis and, therefore, the need for spinal surgery. A hard body orthosis is rigid and does not usually allow for movement of the trunk, in order to hold the body (and, therefore, the scoliosis) as still as necessary. Wearing of the hard TLSO can also sometimes be combined with therapy to help to increase the flexibility of the spine, and counteract the effects of the body being held still within the brace.

Upper limb orthoses

Upper limb orthoses include shoulder, elbow, hand and wrist splints. Similar to the lower limb orthoses, upper limb orthoses are designed to optimise the position and alignment of the bones, muscles and joints of the fingers, hand, wrist, elbow or shoulder.

Elbow splints are generally used to hold the elbow out in a straight or more straightened position. Your child's therapist might recommend an elbow splint to try to prevent your child's elbow from becoming too tightly bent, or to help them to keep their elbow straight during functional activities such as crawling or standing with their hands held out straight. A finger, hand and/or wrist splint is often used to optimise the position of the fingers, hand or wrist to help your child to better open their hand, or to grasp and manipulate objects.

Seating equipment

Specialised seating equipment, such as activity chairs and recliner chairs, are used for children who cannot yet sit up by themselves, who can sit but not with enough stability to use their hands, or who fatigue quickly and cannot sustain a sitting position for very long. The chair then enables them to use their hands, eyes, and head more easily. For example, using an activity chair might help a child to sit more easily so they can play with toys with their hands, eat more safely, or use their eyes to communicate more easily.

Activity chairs all come with some degree of supportive seating, such as a seat base, seat back, arm rests and foot plates. Most activity chairs also include a tray, which can provide additional postural support, but also provides a place for your child to practise their fine motor skills, their communication skills, and their feeding and eating skills.

Sometimes activity chairs include a 'hi-lo' base, which allows the chair to be raised up high, such as up to a kitchen bench or the dinner table, or brought right down low so your child can sit at floor level with their siblings or their friends from day care or school.

Other activity chairs are more portable and are designed to be used on the go, such as when visiting restaurants, your friend's house, at the park, or as an additional support on an aeroplane seat. Many times we recommend a child has access to both options, so that their ability to sit and their participation is enhanced in all of their environments.

Recliner chairs are usually recommended for children with more significant physical needs, or as an alternative seating option for when your child needs some relaxation time or a position change so that they are not constantly sitting in their wheelchair. These chairs are usually reclined and very supportive, which gives your child the chance to relax with their family and friends.

Standing frames

Standing frames are devices that hold your child in an upright standing position. We usually recommend a child starts using a standing frame at around the time they would otherwise be expected to start standing and walking, which is around 12 to 18 months of age.

Three different types of standing frames are available:
- *Prone standing frames* are standing frames where your child lies down on their tummy in the standing frame, and then the frame is brought to upright. To use a prone standing frame,

your child needs to be able to hold their head upright pretty well when sitting.

- *Supine standing frames* are standing frames where your child lies down on their back in the standing frame, and then the frame is brought to upright. These frames can be used by any child, even if they are not able to hold their head upright when sitting. Supine standing frames are also often used for older children who need to be hoisted into the standing frame (that is, because they can no longer be lifted into the standing frame, or they cannot stand up into the standing frame).

- *Upright standing frames* are much less frequently used, but they are frames that hold your child in a completely upright position. To use an upright standing frame, your child will need to have good head and trunk control, and ideally will be able to stand from a sitting position in order to be able to get into the frame. Upright standing frames are sometimes used for children who are working towards being able to propel themselves forwards in an upright standing frame using a walker around them.

You can also get standing frames that have wheelchair style wheels attached to either side so that they can push themselves around in an upright standing position. These are called mobile standers.

Walking frames

Walking frames are used to support and enable children to be able to take steps and walk with support. Many different types of walking frames are available, but they generally fall into two categories, which relate to where the bulk of the walking frame is positioned – either in front of or behind the body:

- *Posterior walking frames wrap around behind a child and are open in front.* These walking frames promote a more upright standing and walking position, and enable children to be able to walk up to and have easy access to things in their environment, such as tables, toilets and chairs. To be able to use a posterior walking frame, your child needs to be able to pull themselves to a standing position from the floor or step transfer independently or with light supervision from a chair, and be able to take steps holding on with their hands.

- *Anterior walking frames wrap around or are positioned in front of the child.* These frames are used if your child requires more support than a posterior walking frame. Anterior walking frames are useful for children who cannot pull to stand from the floor but can stand up from a chair, and can take steps when provided with lots of support through their arms or trunk. Generally, if using an anterior walking frame, your child will be taking their weight through their forearms rather than their hands. An anterior walking frame enables your child to be able to stand up into the standing frame, and then sit down into a chair from the standing frame when they are finished.

Both posterior and anterior standing frames can come with a large range of postural supports, depending on your child's needs. The walking frames I have described utilise your child's upper limb strength to help them to hold themselves up while they step their feet through. However, not all children can use their arms to hold their body weight and help them to walk. If your child fits this description, more highly supportive walking frames are available that hold your child upright through their trunk and pelvis, and allow your child to walk along without using their arms for support.

Why provide your child with a standing frame or walking frame if they are never going to learn to walk?

For some children, we know from the time of their diagnosis that they are not likely going to be able to walk. For example, I have seen two children in my career who had very severe spina bifida with absolutely no muscle activation in their legs below their thighs. I have also seen a child with a complete spinal cord injury who had no muscle activation or sensation in his legs. I knew these children were not going to learn to stand or walk by themselves. However, we still got these children standing frames. Why did we do this? Because of the benefits of standing and moving in an upright position:

- It brings your child upright so that they can be at the same level as their peers and friends. This supports the development of your child's social, communication, interaction and play skills.
- It helps to keep your child's joints and muscles flexible. If your child is not able to stand at all, they will get tight muscles and joint contractures in their hips, knees and ankles. Standing every day enables your child to stretch out those muscles and joints and helps them maintain the movement available in those joints and muscles.
- It allows your child to take weight through the bones of their pelvis and legs, which is very important to increase your child's bone density and to protect and promote the normal development of their hip joints.
- It helps your child's respiratory and digestive systems, because gravity elongates your child's trunk, supporting their breathing, rib cage development, and digestion of their food.
- Learning to move from one place to another helps your child develop their sense of independence and self-identity, and their ability to make choices about where they can go and who they want to spend time with and what toys or places they want to play. It provides them with a variety of experiences of movement and exploration, which contributes to their cognitive development.

Specialised disability prams

Standard prams available from baby shops have relatively limited postural supports compared to disability-specific prams, which have additional postural supports to allow your child to sit in an upright posture if they cannot do so themselves. Some specialised disability prams are also able to tilt back in space, and can come with a tray your child can use to help them play and use their hands and feed while sitting in the pram.

Manual wheelchairs

Manual wheelchairs require a person to push them, either through self-propelling (the person in the wheelchair is pushing themselves), or through attendant-propelling (another person is pushing the wheelchair from the handles behind). Manual wheelchairs are usually recommended for children who cannot walk but can push themselves, or might be able to walk but cannot walk for long distances or cannot keep up with their peers, or for whom walking is fatiguing so they cannot walk all day or every day. For these children, manual wheelchairs enable them to continue to get around their environment in an energy-efficient way so that they can participate in their everyday life.

Alternatively, manual wheelchairs are also prescribed for children who are not able to drive themselves in a power wheelchair, or as a backup chair for children who can and do drive themselves in a power wheelchair for times when using their power wheelchair is not appropriate or their power wheelchair is broken or being serviced.

Manual wheelchairs come in many different types, styles and configurations, with many different postural or functional components. For example, some manual wheelchairs are able to be tilted back in space, which enables a child to rest if they get fatigued when sitting up for long periods of time, to relieve pressure off their bottoms if required, or for a child's safety during seizures. Your child's occupational therapist or physiotherapist will be able to discuss the features that might be necessary for your child, and will trial chairs to ensure the chair that is prescribed is going to meet your child's needs.

Power wheelchairs

Power chairs are driven using electric motorised power. Power wheelchairs are recommended for children who cannot push themselves in a manual wheelchair, but who will be able to safely drive a power chair to get themselves independently around their own environment. To be able to drive and steer a power wheelchair, your child needs to have some part of their body they can control sufficiently. Most people would be familiar with joystick controlled power chairs, but people can learn to control power wheelchairs with their forehead, their chin, their feet – some researchers are even working on being able to harness a person's brain signals to control the driving of a power wheelchair! However, to safely use a power wheelchair, your child needs to have adequate vision and depth perception, and reasonable cognitive ability to understand safe driving principles.

Pram versus wheelchair

If your child is still young, it can be a big decision as to whether you get them a specialised pram or a wheelchair. Your child's occupational therapist and/or physiotherapist can help to discuss the options and pros and cons for your child and their needs, but here are some general considerations:

- How old is your child? How socially appropriate is it for them to be in a pram? We usually recommend that children who are school aged or approaching school age should probably be considering a wheelchair because it is more age-appropriate for them to be in a wheelchair if they are going to be using the chair full time or more often than not. If your child is very young, a specialised disability pram might be more appropriate. However, if your child is going to eventually learn to push themselves in a wheelchair, we might try to find your child a very small wheelchair or another device to help them learn the basic principles and actions of pushing themselves from place to place in preparation for a wheelchair in the future.

- How often will they be using the pram or wheelchair? For some older children, it might be okay to use a pram if use is infrequent.
- Are you expecting your child will be able to push themselves in a wheelchair eventually? If your child is likely to eventually push themselves in a wheelchair, even over shorter distances, your child using a wheelchair straightaway might be beneficial so that they can learn to safely propel themselves.
- Where and in what circumstances will you be using the pram or wheelchair? The weight, size and durability of the pram or wheelchair need to be considered, as well as the environments in which they need to be used and how you will be transporting the chair, to make sure it will suit your child's lifestyle and the activities they want to participate in while in the chair.

Bath and shower/toilet seats

Bath and shower seats are specially designed to be used for bathing or showering your child, and many are also designed to be used over a toilet. Bath and shower seats are used to support your child's independence, to ensure your child's safety during baths and showers, and to also ensure your safety as a parent when bathing or showering your child. Bath and shower/toilet seats can vary significantly in the amount of support provided, so it is important to discuss your child's needs with a therapist find the most suitable chair or support.

Hoists

A hoist with a sling may be recommended to help you transfer your child from one piece of equipment or position to another once they get too heavy to lift, or if they are difficult to hold safely when transferring them. Hoists generally fall into two categories – mobile hoists or ceiling hoists:

- Mobile hoists are standalone hoists that have a frame on wheels to which the sling attaches, and can be moved by pushing the frame around.

- Ceiling hoists are hoists that are attached to either a single point, or to a track on the ceiling. Ceiling hoists are only able to be used in the location in which they are positioned or, in the case of ceiling tracks, as far as the ceiling track will go. However, ceiling hoists are less bulky, and take up less space in smaller areas.

Switches

Switches are electronic buttons that your child can press to make something happen. Switches are great for children with limited motor control to learn cause and effect, and also for them to be able to communicate. For example, your child might use a switch to be able to scan through and select a word from a series of words so that they can ask you something, or put some words together to tell you what they want to tell you. Switches and the technology available for switch access is now very advanced, and switches can be used for even very complex technological activities such as working on computers or other devices, controlling the environment in which we live (for example, turning on and off lights, air conditioning and appliances, and opening and closing doors), and for recreational activities such as electronic gaming and driving drones!

Augmentative Alternative Communication devices

Augmentative Alternative Communication (AAC) devices assist a person to communicate their messages. AACs can be either low-tech or high-tech:

- Low-tech devices include printed communication boards, communication books or communication pictures that do not require the use of technology. However, sometimes low tech devices can require the use of a communication partner (someone who assists with delivering the message or turning the pages or helping the person to select their request), which means the person is not as independent as they would be if they did not need a communication partner.

- High-tech devices include programs on an iPad or a computer, and standalone specialised electronic communication devices, which enable the user to select their message to be delivered by the communication device to the receiver. As discussed in the beginning of this chapter, communication devices, regardless of whether they are low-tech or high-tech, enable a greater amount of independence with communicating with others, for the purpose of increased interaction, independence, and capacity to participate, learn and, ultimately, to contribute.

Last thoughts on assistive technology

When one of the therapists in my team asks me if we should trial a piece of equipment with a child – assuming the suggestion is not outrageously inappropriate – my answer is often, 'Why not?' Why shouldn't we give children every opportunity to learn to move, play, interact, make choices and develop any skills available to them? And even if, in the end, their attempts to learn these skills are not successful, at least we have tried, and the child will have gained many other benefits out of the process. And you, as a parent, will feel confident that you have tried all you can to help your child to become as independent as possible.

Assisting, but not insisting, summary points

- The overall purpose of childhood is to help your child to become as independent as possible. You will need to find a balance between giving your child the help they need, and also supporting them to become as independent as possible.

- The ability to make choices is a fundamental skill that will help your child to develop their independence.

- Let your child initiate movements or activities. Self-initiated movement is essential to early choice making. Treatment should be done with your child, not to your child.

- To learn, refine and master new skills, your child needs repetition of practice in a variety of ways and situations to help them move towards becoming more independent in their everyday activities.

- Assistive technology or equipment is designed to assist your child to develop their abilities and become as independent as possible so they can show just how capable they are.

Part IV: Validate your child

The overall purpose of the development of any child, and of childhood, is to prepare them for their life ahead as an adult. The exact same purpose applies for your child with different needs or a disability. You want your child to grow up to be a happy, fulfilled and loved adult. So what is it that children need to become happy, fulfilled and loved adults?

Up until now we have covered off on starting to help your child as early as possible (being aware), making sure you understand and take steps to meet their needs across all areas (recognising your child's needs), and helping your child to become as independent as possible (assisting, but not insisting). The next part to understand is validating your child – helping them to understand who they are as a person, outside of their developmental delay or disability.

I mentioned Zach Anner, an American author and comedian, earlier in the book. Zach has quadriplegic cerebral palsy, and uses a power wheelchair for his mobility. If you check out Zach's social media pages and YouTube channel, you will see he has some very key messages about the importance of allowing your child to develop their sense of identity by allowing them to give things a go, presuming they are capable, and allowing them to follow their own dreams and passions.

Zach's 'Workout Wednesday' clips are funny and insightful, and demonstrate Zach's attitude of 'why not?' when it comes to his own capabilities. Within his book *If at birth you don't succeed: my adventures with disaster and destiny*, Zach recalls how the attitude of his parents first instilled in him a can-do attitude:

> *When I was born, those who didn't know me would have called my circumstances a tragedy. But my parents knew better. When they looked at me, what they saw was just a kid who was destined to take a different path than that of anyone else they'd known. They gave me the tools to explore and let me find my own identity.*

For someone who has what would normally be described as quite a significant physical disability, Zach is a pretty independent guy who has done more in his life than most of us. He has met Oprah, has written and produced his own TV shows, written a book and travelled the world. He lives independently, has participated in a multitude of sports, is a spokesperson for people with disability, and a paid speaker – pretty impressive for a guy in his thirties.

In the chapters in this part, we explore some ideas and strategies that you can adopt to help your child discover who they are in this world, regardless of their diagnosis or disability. Discovering who they are involves your child developing their own unique self-identity and developing a sense of competence in themselves – that feeling that they are capable and useful and have value to offer others. It involves your child developing connections with others so they can understand who they are in relation to other people, and helping them to develop their own story about themselves so that they can help other people to understand who they are and what they are capable of. By helping your child develop a strong sense of themselves, your child will be able to continue their lives being happy, fulfilled and connected.

CHAPTER TWELVE

Developing self-identity and competence

As a parent, you have a profound influence on your child and how they view the world, their position in the world, and their own capabilities. Helping your child to develop their sense of self – their self-identity – enables them to grow into a confident, brave and capable adult who can direct and lead their own life.

The extent of your child's physical or cognitive difficulties doesn't matter – developing their self-identity and the ability to show value to others is essential. This chapter will take you through what is self-identity, the importance of the development of self-identity to your child's safety and wellbeing, some strategies that you can use to allow your child to develop their self-identity, and ways you and your child can teach others to presume competence in your child.

Allow self-identity to develop

What is self-identity? It is our answer to 'who am I?' Our self-identity can be an expression of who we are in relation to other people, our roles within life (including personal or work-related roles), our personality attributes, our understanding of our skills and capabilities, our morals and values, and our interests, passions or hobbies. It can also change over time and in response to events we experience. For example, if I were to answer the question 'who am I?' my response could comprise of any of the following:

- A mother, wife, sister, daughter, friend (my relationship to others).
- A physiotherapist and business owner (my professional or work-related roles).
- A former competitive swimmer, who now tries to remain fit in among all the other things in adult life (my personal interests).
- Fiercely independent, a people pleaser, can be a bit sentimental (my personality traits).
- Usually organised, but sometimes untidy (my habits).
- Strong belief that as a society we should be supporting each other (my worldview, morals, values).

Depending on the context in which I am thinking about my self-identity, my response might vary, but I still have a reasonably strong sense of myself and my preferences in life. This has helped me to make decisions that are in line with my values and morals, and to pursue things of interest to me, which helps me to feel a sense of fulfilment.

Like us, children develop their sense of self-identity through a multitude of ways, including the things they are told by us, their parents, and other people in their lives, their opportunities and experiences in life, and the culture and environment they live in. They also develop their self-identity through the choices they get to make and the lessons learnt from those choices, by being given a chance to have a go at things and either succeeding or learning to fail and developing resilience. And, finally, they develop their self-identity through their connections and relationships with others, by participating in activities and being part of a community, and by being given opportunities to follow their own interests and passions.

For children who have a developmental delay or disability, their sense of self is in some part going to be affected by their disability. However, this chapter focuses on the other ways you can help your child develop their self-identity and, in particular, develop a strong and positive sense of themselves that they can take with them into their future. Your child's self-identity is something that you have significant influence over, but also something you need to give them a chance to develop. Helping your child to develop their sense of self might involve you stepping back, and giving them the opportunity to figure out their way in the world by themselves. The majority of this chapter takes you through strategies you can try with your child to help them develop a strong sense of who they believe themselves to be.

Importance of self-identity to safety and wellbeing

Before we move onto the strategies, I want to take a moment to point out the importance of your child's self-identity to their safety and wellbeing. Your child's development of their self-identity includes the development of a sense of their value and worthiness of attention and care. Intrinsically linked to this sense of value is the development of personal boundaries and being able to speak up if they feel that their boundaries are at risk of being, or have been, compromised. A boundary is the preferences or rules your child has about things that happen to them. The boundaries your child has will include physical boundaries – that is, what happens to them physically – as well as moral or personal boundaries – that is, how they expect to be treated, how they believe they should treat others, and behaviours they believe are acceptable or unacceptable, both towards themselves and towards others.

Your child having a strong sense of self and a strong self-identity is important, along with a strong sense of their own personal boundaries, and what constitutes a breach of these boundaries. In addition, having a strong self-identity can give your child the confidence to speak up or ask for help when they feel they need it, which can help to maintain your child's safety and wellbeing – both in a physical and a mental or moral sense. This is particularly important for children with physical or cognitive needs who will potentially rely on other people in their daily life to assist with their daily needs. As you can see, your child's self-identity is essential for them to manage their own safety and wellbeing as best they can, to have the confidence to say yes or no to activities, events or statements from others, or to reach out for help from someone they trust if they feel their safety or wellbeing is being compromised.

Foster independence

Helping your child to develop their sense of independence is so important to them developing an understanding of who they are by themselves, away from you or the other people in their life who help them. This is especially important for children who do rely on physical assistance in their everyday life.

Developing or fostering independence supports your child to understand that they *are* capable, that they *can* learn to do things, that they *can* help themselves, and that they *do* have something of value they can offer to others.

Letting your child have a go first

To help foster independence, let your child have a go at something, even if you don't think they can do it. This shows them you are willing to let them try, and you believe they have the capacity to do something. If your child does not achieve the task by themselves, the following sections provide a few options.

Developing self-identity and competence

Count to 5 (or 10, or 20)

Sometimes our children just need more time to figure things out for themselves. This can be hard for us parents in this busy day and age. I know I have been guilty of doing things for my kids just because I can do it quicker, or because I don't have time to teach them to do their shoes up because I need to get out the door before we're running late for something. You might also have other reasons for wanting to do things for your child, rather than letting them have a go or waiting for them to try themselves. You might not want to see them fail. You might not want them to get frustrated and disappointed in themselves. You might not want them to realise that there are going to be things in their lives that they find difficult or impossible to do as a result of their disability.

However, giving your child an opportunity to try to do something for themselves allows them to recognise that they have the capacity to try. Trying and failing also increases their resilience (more on that in 'Let your child fail', later in this chapter). But even more so, some children with developmental delays and disabilities actually need more time to process the information they have received before they can achieve the action themselves. For example, we have one little girl we see in our clinic who is two years old and has a severe cortical malformation resulting in severe cerebral palsy. We have been working with this little girl on her ability to interact with others. We are doing this by scratching on a board, and waiting for her to respond by scratching back, or by copying sounds she makes and then waiting for her to respond in turn. When we first started out working with this little girl, her therapist had to wait 40 seconds after they scratched or made a sound before she was able to respond in turn. 40 seconds! And in that 40 seconds, all her therapist did was wait ... They didn't prompt her, didn't make any more noises or scratches, and didn't try to change activities (which can be tempting because it is easy to think after waiting 40 seconds that the child is just not interested in the activity that we are doing). For a parent, 40 seconds is a long time if you are in a rush. However, this girl needed those

40 seconds to process the information she was receiving, integrate that information, and formulate her response – which was to scratch back or make a noise in response.

Obviously, you may not be able to wait 40 seconds every time you want to give your child a chance to do something (none of us would ever get to work on time if we had to!). But a good trick is to count, SLOWLY, to 5 or 10 or 20 in your head, to allow your child the time they need to respond. If you notice your child becomes distracted, then you have given them too long and they have disengaged from the activity you have been trying to get them to do. Find the length of time it takes your child to respond and have a go, and wait that amount of time before giving them a hand. (As a side note, this girl got better and better at processing and responding to information, and her response time eventually decreased to five seconds.)

Demonstrating and copying

This is a process of showing your child how to do something or modelling a behaviour, and then getting them to copy your actions. Children learn a lot from us through observation. You can either show them and they try to do the task at the same time, or you can do it first and then they copy you afterwards. Demonstrating or modelling is a good strategy to use for tasks that have a series of simple steps (such as packing away toys, washing a cup or feeding a pet). It is also a good strategy if your child has difficulties with following verbal instructions, or to teach skills that are hard to explain in words (such as empathy or body language). If your child is able to copy your demonstrations, you might also be able to progress to using visual prompts for tasks that your child is familiar with, but might require a reminder to complete all the steps. This is a great tool for use with everyday self-care tasks like toileting, brushing teeth, or preparing a meal. By having a visual prompt of the steps required for the task, your child can more independently follow them and complete the task themselves.

Backwards chaining

This involves doing all the steps of a process except for the last step, which your child then completes. Once your child has mastered the last step in a process, you complete all steps of the process except for the last two steps. And then the last three steps and so on. For example, if you are teaching your child to put a shirt on, you will put it over their head, help them to pull their arms through (talking them through each step), and then ask them to pull the shirt down over their tummy as the last step. Once your child has mastered that, you might then teach them to put one arm through the sleeve and pull the shirt down over their tummy. Gradually, over a series of steps, your child will learn all the steps in the task until they can complete the full task.

Task analysis and coaching

This involves looking at a task, thinking through what steps are needed to complete it, analysing how to do those steps, and then guiding or coaching your child through those steps. For example, when learning to tie their shoelaces, you can break the task down into a series of discrete steps that you then teach your child (for example, tie a knot, make a bunny ear, wrap the other lace around the bunny ear, push the lace through the hole, then hold both loops and pull firm). Ideally, you would complete this task analysis and coaching with your child, so that your child can develop some ownership over their choice of how the task is completed.

Step-by-step motor planning

This is similar to the preceding process of task analysis and coaching, but may involve more complex breakdown of the task and analysis of the movements and motor activities required to complete the tasks. Task analysis and motor planning is often required for children with cerebral palsy or cognitive impairments who have difficulties with planning their movements, and require cuing and cognitive practice of these tasks to achieve them.

Allow your child to experience mastery

Mastery is defined as:

- comprehensive knowledge or skill in a particular subject or activity

- control or superiority over someone or something.

For your child with a developmental delay or disability, developing and experiencing mastery involves exploring their capabilities and helping them to become comprehensively competent at something.

Find how your child can be useful – even if they are unable to do most things another child can do. Your job is to find purpose and meaning for your child's life. What is it that your child *can* do? Can they help to hold the bowl for you while you mix the biscuit mixture? Can they choose which song they want to listen to next? Can they listen to the book when you are reading? Find the activities that your child can do or contribute to, and make sure they have opportunity to do it. By doing so, you can create purpose and meaning for your child, and a sense of contribution and accomplishment.

Choosing 'just right' challenges

Part of helping your child to experience mastery involves you choosing 'just right' challenges – that is, challenges that are just hard enough that your child has to work a little to achieve, but also not too hard that they are not able to complete them.

Like any child, your child may get frustrated or bored if the activities or tasks we ask them to complete are either too hard or too easy. Choosing a just right challenge requires you to think about what they are currently capable of, and choosing a new task or an extension of a task that they might find a little challenging, but that they are also definitely capable of achieving. The just right challenge also needs to be an activity or task that your child is motivated to persist with or have a go at. If your child is not interested in achieving the activity or task, they will not be motivated to persist, and so will choose to opt out earlier than if they were interested in the activity.

The other aspect of choosing the just right challenge for your child is choosing one that is not too exciting. For some children with motor or sensory difficulties, and particularly children with neurological or neurodevelopmental conditions, choosing an activity that is very exciting or stimulating can increase their muscle tone and spasticity or their sensory load, which then decreases their ability to control their movements or behaviours. We see this all the time in therapy sessions, so we have to be careful when selecting the just right challenge for each child, or quickly modify an activity or task if the child we are working with becomes too excited or overwhelmed by the activity.

Case study

Victor is a four-year-old boy with cerebral palsy that affects his arms, legs and trunk. When Victor is practising standing up and reaching, it is important that he is doing this with control. However, which toy we choose to encourage Victor to stand will change how well he can stand with control. If we choose something that is exciting or funny, such as a toy that he can knock off his dad's head, or a loud toy that makes a funny noise, Victor will get too excited and will start to use the spasticity and tone in his legs to stand instead of using controlled activation of his muscles and a controlled movement pattern. In comparison, if we choose something like a book, or a simple song, Victor is more likely to stand up with control because his excitement does not take over.

Another personal example I have experienced is choosing the just right activity when encouraging your child to learn to use a pencil and draw. One day when I was sitting with my son while he was drawing, I thought I would take the opportunity to try to challenge his drawing and copying skills. At that stage, he was just scribbling randomly with the pencil, so I picked up a pencil and showed him how to draw a single straight line (one of the earlier things children usually copy). I demonstrated drawing the line a couple of times,

> and then asked him if he wanted to have a go. He copied a line or two, so I thought I would show him a circle. I demonstrated the circle, and then offered for him to have a go. While he initially attempted to draw a circle shape, it was quite difficult for him. As a result, he got frustrated, and ended up choosing to stop using the pencil and instead thought it would be fun to spread the pencils all over the table.

Let your child fail

Letting your child fail is an important part of life, and of developing mastery and resilience. Part of problem-solving is learning to fail at things, and using that failure to refine any future attempts. Many parents of children with disabilities are careful not to let their child experience failure. And I can understand this – your child already has enough hardship in their life, and you want to avoid them having to go through more. However, failure as a result of trying and life generally being difficult are two separate things. Your child having a go at something and failing teaches them to pick themselves back up again and have another go. This teaches them to be resilient. And being resilient is important for children with disabilities who are going to come across difficulties in their life that they will either need to overcome or learn to accept.

Notice the wording of this section: let or letting. The word 'let' means to allow, let go and allow to happen, which indicates a release of control. How can you, as a parent whose child depends upon you for help with things in their life, 'let go' or release control? The following sections in this chapter provide some help.

Ask 'Why Not?'

When considering whether your child might be able to try something, my approach, and the approach my team adopts, is 'Why not?' Who are we to determine what your child's capabilities are? By presuming your child has the capability to do something, we will presume that

Developing self-identity and competence

your child might very well be able to drive that power wheelchair, or walk in a supportive walker, or participate in wheelchair basketball, or attend a mainstream school, or so on and so on. Because without giving your child the opportunity to try, how will we know for sure what they are capable of?

As clinicians, the 'why not?' approach relates to what we can try to help your child do in therapy. As a parent, the 'why not?' approach relates to what opportunities you give your child to try at home and when they are out with you or others in community. Taking a 'why not?' approach requires a solutions-focused attitude. Instead of looking for what barriers exist to your child being able to do something, you need to figure out how you can make it happen.

Here are some questions you can use to help you unpack the opportunities available in a situation, and so feel confident when making a 'why not?' decision for your child:

- Is the activity reasonably within their capabilities, or closely within range of their capabilities? If your child has emerging or established skills that will enable them to give the activity a good go, then 'why not?'

- Is the activity something you think is well outside their capabilities? If so, how can you adapt or modify the activity to enable your child to have a go? For example, if your child wants to have a go at riding their bike to school, but you know they will have difficulties with making the distance, you could drive them halfway and then ride together from there.

- Is having a go or trying an activity going to cause your child harm (either physically or mentally)? If the activity is physically or mentally unsafe for your child, obviously it is important you manage that risk. However, I would encourage you to then also ask yourself (and also ask your child if that is appropriate) how you can modify or adapt the activity to make it safe for them to try. If you can include your child in that problem-solving process, they too can develop a 'why not?' approach to having a go at things in life.

I have many stories about children who have proven our assumptions to be wrong, and to be honest, these are probably my favourite stories to share. These are not stories of miracle cures or miraculous outcomes – they are just stories showing that, if you give a child an opportunity to have a go at something, despite some reservations, they might very well prove that they are more capable than we had originally anticipated.

Case study

Shaun is a young man with severe cerebral palsy affecting his trunk and all four of his limbs, who I met when he was 10 years old. Shaun had poor eye movements and lots of obligatory movement patterns that he cannot control, but which he uses functionally to reach and look. As a young boy, as a result of these limited movement patterns, his therapist was worried that he would not be able to drive a power wheelchair. To look forwards, he would turn his head to the side and then look out the side of his eye. Because he constantly had his head turned to one side, his therapist was unsure whether he would be able to see sufficiently to be able to drive, and also to use his hands with enough control to be able to steer the joystick of the power wheelchair. However, his therapist had a 'why not?' attitude, and so took Shaun to a large empty shopping centre car park, put him into an old power wheelchair, and let him have a go. And despite the visual and motor difficulties, Shaun learnt to independently drive the power wheelchair, and now uses one independently within his home and community.

Lilly is a young girl, also with severe cerebral palsy, also affecting her trunk, arms and legs. Lilly cannot hold her head upright for any longer than a few seconds. She has very uncontrolled movements of her arms and legs, and has severely limited ability to move her body – essentially all she can do without help from others is to roll onto one side. However, Lilly's mum really wanted to see if she could walk in a supportive walking frame. We were not sure if we would be able to find a frame supportive enough, but we adopted our 'why not?' attitude and talked to an equipment supplier who we knew would be solutions-focused in finding something to work for this little girl. At the trial, the equipment supplier was able to rig up a head rest and head support for a highly supportive walking frame, and this little girl was able to take steps with the walker. Her mum cried tears of joy to see her little girl up and walking. She could now experience being upright with her little sister and initiate movement from one place to another, and do this independently without the help of her parents, carers or therapists. This outcome, in my view, is priceless.

Presume competence

Behind every young child who believes in himself is a parent who believed first.
Matthew Jacobson

The most important thing you can do for your child is to presume they are capable – capable to do things, make decisions, understand what is being said to them and what is happening to them, and capable of joy and pleasure and fulfilment.

Presuming competence is a key approach that we adopt when working with children with disabilities, and something we try to instil in all the other people involved in your child's life. Presuming competence includes presuming your child, or any child or person with a disability, can hear and understand what is being said to them. It includes presuming your child can achieve the goals they set out to achieve. It includes presuming your child might reasonably be able to do something.

Ways your child's carers and therapists can presume competence with your child include the following:

- Greet your child and look at them when they talk to them, and teach others to do the same.

- Explain what is going to happen to your child so that they can hear it before they do it.

- Ask your child for permission to do something to them before they do it.

- Give your child opportunities to communicate in any way they can, and recognise and respect their attempts at communication.

- Give your child time to respond. As covered earlier in this chapter, your child may require increased processing time to be able to respond to a question or direction or interaction. Alternatively, if your child has not previously been presumed to be competent, it might take them some time to realise that they have been given permission to give something a go.

- Allow your child to have a go at a task even if the carer or therapist doesn't think they can do it, or that they can't do it well, or that they can't do it neatly/fast enough/carefully enough/100 per cent successfully.

Because you spend more time with your child than anyone else, you are the best person to understand your child's competence, and also to give them opportunities to explore their competence in a safe and supportive environment. When presuming and giving your child opportunity to demonstrate their competence, it is important to be okay with whatever the outcome of their attempt is, to have patience, and to be supportive and encouraging, no matter how successful or unsuccessful your child's attempt may have been. As already touched on, this can be tough! All parents struggle to let their child attempt a task or activity without trying to control their child's performance – whether that be through constantly giving instructions or feedback, taking over the task or activity at the first sign of difficulty or the child not doing it the way the parent had envisioned, or saying passively negative comments at the end like, 'Oh, well, maybe you will get it next time'. As a parent, it is important to let go of some of your preconceived ideas about how a task should typically be done,

Developing self-identity and competence

and just let your child take some time to figure out how they are going to do it.

A common example of needing to let go of control is when the task of decorating the Christmas tree comes round, with many parents (sooner or later) recognising they have to let go of how this task is done in order to allow their child develop their sense of competence and mastery. I know I am not alone in the group of parents who cringe and struggle to watch as their children place all the decorations on one branch or section of the tree, instead of spacing them out evenly and symmetrically as I would prefer. The same situation occurs every time I let my four year old decorate a cake – I have to let go of my perception of how the sprinkles or smarties on the cake 'should' look, and just let my daughter decorate it the way she wants to.

Give your child responsibilities

Once you can understand what your child is capable of, you can use those capabilities to give them responsibilities. Responsibilities provide your child with a sense of purpose, but also teach them important life skills such as independence, being dependable to others, being accountable for their behaviour and when meeting commitments, contributing to their family or community, and learning and understanding about consequences when responsibilities are not upheld or maintained.

You can start giving your child responsibilities as soon as they are capable of contributing in any way to a task or activity. To start with, you might only give your child one simple section of the task to complete themselves, such as letting go of the toy to drop it into the toy box when you are packing away at the end of the day. Or they can help you with a task that you are doing, such as pressing the button to turn the washing machine on. As your child's capabilities increase, you can increase the difficulty of the task or the complexity of the task in line with your child's abilities. So, for example, you might progress from just pressing the button to turn on the washing machine, to then reaching to close the door and then pressing the button (which also uses the backwards chaining approach discussed earlier in this chapter). Or your child can start to be responsible for packing away all their toys at the end of the day, instead of doing this with your help.

It is important to ensure you choose an appropriate type and number of tasks that are reasonable for your child to manage so that the responsibilities are possible for your child to meet. It is also important to praise and thank your child whenever they help out or meet their responsibilities. This reinforces to your child that their contribution is valued.

Giving your child feedback about their performance

Part of helping your child develop their competence also relies on you, and your child's therapists and teachers, and how you give feedback to your child when they are attempting a task. The way you deliver feedback, including the words and tone you use, the timing of your feedback, and your child's involvement in the feedback process, all contribute to whether the feedback given assists your child to develop a positive or negative self-identity.

Here are some strategies to providing feedback that assists your child in developing their own competence and a positive sense of self:

- *Before you give feedback, make sure the intention of your feedback to your child is positive.* If no constructive reason for the feedback exists, it is probably better not to give feedback at all.
- *Make sure you are not feeling frustrated, exasperated, stressed or impatient.* Your underlying mood can affect the way you end up delivering feedback to your child.
- *Give praise or positive feedback where it is due.* Don't just point out where your child had difficulties.
- *Be specific, and focus on the behaviours or abilities your child demonstrated.* Did your child try really hard? Did they sit very still? Did they count to the right number they were supposed

Developing self-identity and competence

to? Did they manage to do one loop of their shoelace? What specific part of the activity did your child manage to do well? And what specific part of the activity did they struggle with? Did they get stuck when it was time to loop the second shoelace through? Did they get distracted when noises started outside? Did they lose their hold on the fork when their hand got tired?

- *If your child is older or has good reasoning skills, ask your child how they think they went first, and what they could do differently next time to improve their performance.* This gives your child opportunity to self-reflect first and to self-identify how they could improve, rather than relying on you or other people for all their feedback.

- *Provide strategies to assist with improvement.* Be specific with the strategies, and introduce one strategy at a time. Providing feedback about too many areas at once can overwhelm your child and might make them feel like trying again is pointless.

- *Praise effort as well as achievement.* Praising effort encourages your child to have a go another time. If you just praise achievement, they will not be motivated to try anything unless they know they are going to have success, which will result in them self-limiting their own abilities.

- *Don't give feedback constantly while your child is attempting a task.* Be patient, and give your child time to have a go, problem-solve, and think through ways they might be able to correct or improve their performance themselves. Learning through practice and problem-solving will give your child an even greater sense of competence than just learning through us giving them feedback.

Learning to change your feedback style can take time. Sometimes our feedback style is moulded from quite early, and from how our own parents or other significant people in our lives gave us feedback. So it is important to not be too hard on yourself if you get it wrong sometimes, and to continually reflect and be aware of how you give feedback and the impact that is having on your child.

If you happen to come across a therapist or teacher who does not give feedback to your child in a positive way, it is important that you don't put up with that just because 'they are the expert'. As you will have understood from reading this far into this book, your child's development involves more than learning new physical or cognitive tasks. If learning those physical or cognitive tasks comes at the expense of your child's self-esteem and self-identity, it might not actually be worthwhile. Consider it this way – if your child develops the ability to speak more loudly so they can be heard in the classroom, that skill won't be used to your child's full potential if your child has not also developed the confidence and the competence to use this in their everyday life.

Case study

I have worked with a beautiful family for many years whose child has cerebral palsy. They chose to attend a different service for an intensive block of therapy using a specific approach that has potential to assist children with cerebral palsy. Unfortunately, the person delivering this therapy service had really negative ways of delivering feedback. Some of the comments made included, 'Come on, you're being lazy' or yelling at the child (who was five at the time) to try to motivate them through negative feedback. The overall impact of this experience was that the child came to really dislike therapy, the child and the mother would be in tears during the sessions, and it took a long time for us to earn the trust of this child again afterwards. This is an example of where the way feedback is delivered to a child can have a significant impact on their overall capabilities and their sense of competence.

Developing self-identity and competence

Teaching your child to ask for help

All of us, regardless of whether we have a disability or not, will need help at some point in our lives, and we all have to learn when it is we feel comfortable asking for that help. Part of developing your child's self-identity and competence also requires your child learning when and how to ask for help. Your child with a developmental delay or disability is going to need to ask for help, possibly more so than a child with typical development, in order for them to reach their full potential. And being able to ask for help if and when they need it will help your child to maintain their independence and control of their life, which in turn will help them to develop a strong sense of self-identity.

Case study

As a student I spent four weeks on clinical placement with a community-based spinal injuries support service. During that placement I worked with the therapists to help support a young man who had recently been discharged from the hospital and had moved into a house in the community following his spinal cord injury. This young man had a very high spinal cord injury in his neck, which meant that he had almost no control over the movements of his body, arms and legs. Prior to his spinal cord injury, this man was living independently and working, and was in some sense 'the master of his own universe'. Now he required assistance for almost all physical aspects of his life (such as transfers, dressing, toileting and feeding) although he could drive his power wheelchair independently and use his hands independently to be able to use devices such as his phone – and he was as bright as he ever was. This man had moved into a house where he was going to live by himself, with carers coming to assist him with the tasks he needed to manage in his daily life. He was able to develop his independence and self-identity about who he was now that he had

had a spinal cord injury by being able to organise and direct his own care and help, in the way he wanted it. His ability to ask for help in the way he wanted it was key to him living independently and maintaining his self-identity.

Being able to ask for help provides some important flow-on effects for your child:

- It can help to prevent frustration or disappointment, which in turn can help your child's behaviour and develop their self-identity as someone who can get things done, even if they have to ask for help. As I have mentioned earlier in this book, my son is a bit slow to talk. He has a lot to say, and makes lots of utterances and sounds, but for approximately 50 per cent of the time I cannot figure out what he is talking about (and for other people that percentage would be even higher). Being a typical two year old, he can get frustrated when he cannot do something. For example, if he is trying to climb onto a chair that is a bit high for him, or he is trying to open a particular toy he wants to play with but can't, he can get very frustrated, which results in him getting cranky, yelling, crying, and even sometimes throwing things. To assist him with this, one of the early signs I taught him was the sign for 'help'. Whenever he is getting frustrated, I ask him, 'Do you need help?' and use the sign for help too. He would then sign 'help' back to me, and then I would help him. This process of teaching my son how to ask for help has assisted with decreasing his meltdowns and the tantrums associated with not being able to do something.

- Even though it sounds counterproductive, teaching your child to ask for help will actually assist their sense of competence, through developing their confidence in their ability to give something a go, even if they aren't sure they can achieve it. Teaching your child to be able to ask for help when they need it gives them a backup plan for situations when they try to do something but it is not easy or it does not work out the way they expected. Knowing they can always ask for help enables them to push their own boundaries and challenge their own abilities. This helps them to be able to take risks, which helps them to learn even more about themselves and what they are capable of, and also about consequences of risk-taking. Ultimately, teaching your child to be able to ask for help means your child's abilities can be challenged so that they can reach their full potential. The flipside is, if your child does not learn to challenge their own capabilities and to ask for help if they need it, they can develop a degree of learned dependency – an attitude in which they will rely on others for more than what is necessary, and they become dependent on others for things that they otherwise would be capable of doing for themselves.

Teaching others to presume your child's competence

As a parent, you spend more time with your child compared to anyone else. As a result, you will often understand better than anyone else how capable your child is. Part of your role as a parent is to demonstrate to others how they too can presume competence in your child. Earlier in this chapter I listed some strategies you can use to assume competence in your child. You can model these same strategies to other people to help them to understand your child's capabilities so that they too can presume your child's competence.

Here are some other strategies that might come in handy when helping other people to realise your child's current and potential competence:

- *Educate other people about your child's capabilities, especially people who are just getting to know your child.* You can do this through meetings with new teachers or service providers to discuss your child's capabilities, or putting together an 'About Me' booklet that you can share with people who are getting to know your child.

- *Explain how your child achieves things.* Your child might have developed a unique way to independently complete a task, one that another person who does not know your child as well will not be familiar with. If that person does not know how your child does that task, they may not provide the right environment or set up for your child to be able to do the task, which may result in them assuming your child cannot do it. Sharing any unique strategies or processes your child follows that allow them to be independent will allow other people to know what to expect and allow your child the opportunity to do the activity 'their way'.

- *Explain strategies your child might use to get out of doing things.* Children, even children with disabilities, are very good at using strategies to get out of doing things that are challenging or uninteresting. I have certainly come across children who will purposely cry to try and avoid doing therapy, and one child who would pretend to fall asleep! If another person is unaware of these 'tactics', your child might be able to 'pull the wool over their eyes' and that person's expectations of them will be lower than what your child is actually capable of. Make sure you share these strategies with other people so that they can correctly interpret when your child's actions are genuine – for example, they are genuinely upset or tired – or they are just trying to get out of doing something.

- *Model or demonstrate to others how they might be able to assist your child.* People unfamiliar to your child will take a lot of guidance from you about what your child is capable of. In your everyday interactions with your child, you will be demonstrating to other people the strategies you use with your child to help them to be as capable and independent as possible. If you see someone having difficulty with knowing what your child is capable of, take the initiative to assist that person to understand and learn the strategies you use to help your child to be as competent and capable as possible.

Developing self-identity and competence

Give your child a story or an explanation to re-tell to others

Children are curious creatures, and when children are little, no question is off limits. For your child with a disability, that will include questions from their peers about them. 'What is that on your leg?' 'Why do you have to use a brace on your leg?' 'Why do you have to use a wheelchair?' 'Why can't you talk?' 'Can you play with me?' At a young age, these questions are more often than not just another child being curious about your child's differences, the same as they are curious about any other person's differences. The important thing for your child is that they know how to respond to these questions. Not having an understanding of their disability and not knowing how to answer these questions can leave your child feeling anxious, unsure of themselves and vulnerable. As for anyone, knowledge and understanding is a powerful tool for your child to have when it comes to answering questions like these.

When we first give a child a pair of ankle foot orthoses (AFOs), for example, or when a child with AFOs is about to enter later day care, kindy or prep age, I often have a direct conversation with the child and their parents about what they are going to say to their friends and other kids at school when they ask about their new AFOs. We sometimes rehearse various options of how to respond to that question so the child can find something they understand that feels easy for them to say. The main thing is that the child is prepared for the questions that are going to come. Understanding and being prepared for these questions also allows your child to learn to 'own' their disability, to 'own' the differences that they experience, and develop confidence in themselves. If your child can deliver a 'matter of fact' explanation about why they wear an AFO on their leg, or why they use a wheelchair or use a communication device, then, at a young age, most children will just accept that and move on with enjoying your child's company and accepting them as part of their peer group or friendship group. I have certainly seen this in my child's day care centre, where a little guy in a wheelchair is just part of the kindy group. He is loved and accepted as one of their peers, just like every other child in the classroom, and it is beautiful to see.

Find a balance

Find a balance with your child – yes, they need therapy to help them to do things. But your child is also a child who needs to experience all the 'normal' things that children do. Your child needs time and space to be by themselves. Your child needs to just play freely, without someone directing their movements or activities (and if your child has significant impairments, we need to be able to set up the environment so that they can move and play freely). Your child needs to spend time with you and their siblings so that they can develop these relationships. Your child needs to spend time with others to develop relationships with others. Your child needs to just get out and experience the world. If you spend your whole time doing therapy, attending appointments and so on, your child does not get the chance to develop their understanding of who they are and what their life means. This can result in two things: a very passive child who does not actively participate in their life and who is potentially capable of doing much more than what they actually do, and a very tired, burnt out and emotionally and physically drained family (more about that in the next chapter).

CHAPTER THIRTEEN

Helping your child connect with others

Connecting with others is important to your child's sense of self and acceptance and ability to cope in the world. As humans, we are naturally social and connected beings. Our connections with others help us to feel regulated, safe and engaged with our world, and we seek out these connections with others as much as fulfilling our other basic human needs such as shelter and water. In the movie *Cast Away* that starred Tom Hanks, the drive for human connection to assist with coping in our everyday life can be powerfully seen. In case you haven't seen it (or to refresh your memory), Tom Hanks's character in the movie, Chuck, is left stranded on an uninhabited island after his plane crashes into the Pacific Ocean. Chuck survives for four years on the island, with no human contact at all during that time. However, in some respects, Chuck does maintain a connection of a sort during his lone four years that helps him to cope with the difficulties he faces – he changes a hand mark on a Wilson brand volleyball into a face, names the volleyball 'Wilson' and starts talking to it. Chuck's connection with this volleyball helps him to cope during stressful, challenging or difficult times. Chuck has forged a way to experience connection with another thing, despite his circumstances of being on an uninhabited island.

Being able to connect with others can help your child understand who they are in the world and their relationships with others, and draw upon those connections in order to build resilience and capabilities. This chapter explores some key ways your child can build connections with others – through simply being with others and interacting with others, and through participation, pursuing their passions, and sports and physical activity.

Simply being with others

The first level of connecting with others is simply to be with another person. Even though it does not sound like very much, simply being with others has important implications for your child's development.

If we think about all babies, typically developing or otherwise, all babies enter this world with the innate ability to 'be with others', and draw power from that connection with others. Newborn babies have a strong emotional connection with their parents, as well as other familiar caregivers. Babies also derive a lot of physical and emotional stability from simply being held by others, which requires minimal social interaction – through the simple connection of touch, warmth, physical contact, voice and rocking, babies can be settled. In a reciprocal fashion, parents can also derive immense satisfaction, and a sense of safety, gratitude and love just by being with their babies.

As a new parent, with both of my kids, I remember sneaking into their rooms at night and sleeping on the floor by their cots, because I would yearn to be close to them. I am sure I am not the only parent who has done this. This is the power of simply being with another person.

This power can also be seen when someone is upset or grieving. By simply spending time with that person, without necessarily talking or doing anything other than being, we can have a positive impact on that person – they can start to feel like they are not alone, that they are connected to another person, and that someone is there for them. That person can also start to feel calmer and more regulated, which helps them to then be able to think more rationally or cognitively.

Being with another person is why we go to the movies with another person, instead of by ourselves. Even though you don't talk to the person throughout the entire movie, you are experiencing something together, whether that is shared joy, excitement, fear or sadness. And that can enhance your experience of the movie more so than if you had been at the movies by yourself.

Your child can gain the same sense of connection just by being with other people. It is important that your child is given opportunity to spend time with other people in their lives – with you, their siblings, their friends, other people in the community, and even strangers. By being with other people, your child can develop a sense of who they are within the world. And for you, as a parent who is also trying to understand who your child is in the world and what that means for you – taking your child to spend time with others, bringing your child with you to events and activities where possible, and introducing your child to other people, whether they be close friends or strangers, also helps you to develop your own understanding of who your child is within the world. Being able to be with others enables your child to then take steps (figuratively, not always literally) to actively participate in activities, which will further enhance their self-identity.

Interacting with others

An extension of simply being with others is learning to interact with others (and also teaching other people to interact with your child). Being able to interact with others requires for your child to be able to trust and make a connection with other people, understand that they have something to contribute to the interaction, develop a willingness to share and take turns, communicate (using whatever method your child is capable of), and be sensitive to other people's feelings. In addition, to ensure your child's success with interacting with others, you might also need to teach other people how to interact with your child.

As well as the strategies I cover in chapters 10 and 12 on interaction and communication, and on presuming competence and teaching others to presume competence, here are some strategies to support your child to successfully learn to interact with others:

- *Using play to learn social skills:* Play is an ideal way for your child to learn the skills of interacting with others. Play can help your child to practise the skills of joint attention, turn-taking, sharing interests and cooperation with others. Play is also a really nice (and safe) way for you and your child to role-model different behaviours and interactions, and model how these might affect another person's feelings, teaching your child about empathy and being sensitive to other people's feelings. You can do this using toys, hand puppets, or even role-playing with your child.

- *Social stories:* Social stories can be used to help explain social situations, teach expected behaviours or to teach children about certain processes – for example, the steps they need to take to go to the toilet at school. In particular, social stories can be used to teach your child about unfamiliar situations, or to help them to improve their behaviour and interactions in situations in which they are having difficulties. Social stories can be adapted to your child's individual needs, and can be presented visually as pictures or a video, or as an audio recording, and using language or gestures appropriate to your child's abilities.

- *Model for your child how to interact with others:* Demonstrate to your child what social interactions might look like. You can do this with your child, with a toy, or with another child through acting out appropriate behaviour. As an example, when I was pregnant with my second child, I knew my daughter would need to learn how to share my attention and take turns with sitting on my lap. To help her, we practised taking turns with a teddy to sit in my lap.

- *Practise turn-taking:* Taking turns is fundamental to social communication, so practising turn-taking is important for your child to learn to interact successfully with others. Your child may have difficulties with either knowing that they can initiate interaction and have their turn, or with waiting and allowing other people to have a turn. You can help your child to practise initiating their turn by observing and following their interests, letting them lead, and waiting to give them time to initiate the interaction. And you can help your child to learn to take turns using the preceding two strategies (social stories and modelling), and by using games or activities that require turn-taking. Start with a small wait, and build up the wait time as your child gets comfortable with taking turns.

- *Teach other people how they can interact with your child:* Interaction requires the participation of two or more people, so it is just as important to teach other people how to successfully interact with your child as it is to teach your child how to interact with others. Your child might have unique strategies that need to be used to enable successful interaction with others. For example, your child might use a specific communication strategy or tool, make certain sounds to mean certain things, need to have objects or pictures placed in certain fields of their vision, or need time to process information before they are able to respond and take their turn.

Participation

Participation is a word commonly used by therapists or healthcare workers when discussing goals and aspirations you might have for your child; however, it is not always clearly understood by parents (and even by some health professionals). In this section, I will explain what the word 'participation' means and explore ways that you can facilitate your child's participation.

If you look up the definition of participation in the dictionary, you will come up with variations of the following:

- the action of taking part in something
- the act of joining with others in doing something
- the act of taking part in an event or activity.

Synonyms of participation may include involvement, taking part, engagement and contribution.

For children (or adults) with a disability, participation requires two key factors to be met – firstly, being able to access and be in *attendance* at something but, secondly, and more importantly, being actively *involved* in something, whether that be an activity, an event, or a movement or cause.

Understanding why participation is important

Participation (specifically the act of being involved and contributing to something) helps your child develop a sense of confidence and competence, their sense of self, and sense of interest in activities that hold meaning or value.

Participation also contributes to your child's self-determination – their ability to make choices based on their preferences, the things or activities that interest them, or things or activities that hold meaning or value to them at a personal level.

Case study

Justin is a boy who I have worked with for a very long time. Justin is a lovely boy, very polite, very hardworking. He has cerebral palsy that primarily affects his legs. He can walk independently without any aids, but often uses a walker to manage his fatigue and for balance, and uses a wheelchair for longer distances. When Justin was eight years old he participated in his first Pilates class that we were running for children of all abilities. Justin worked hard with his mum's help, and completed the six-week program of classes, improving his strength, flexibility, and alignment. At the end of the program, we handed out to each of the children a medal for them to celebrate the completion of the program. I have never seen someone more proud of themselves than Justin on that day. With this big grin on his face, Justin said to his mum, 'I am so proud of myself'. His mum, the Pilates teacher and I all had smiles on our faces and tears in our eyes seeing how amazingly proud he was of himself. His mum told me later that the next day he wore his medal to school to show all his school mates. Participating in this physical activity program, as well as providing physical benefits, also allowed Justin to develop a sense of accomplishment and pride in his abilities and capacity.

Getting your child involved

Many children with disabilities are able to attend activities or events. Being in attendance means being present, and relies on accessibility. In contrast, *becoming involved* in something or an activity is actually taking part or experiencing being involved.

Attendance or 'being there' can be measured in terms of frequency – for example, how often is your child able to attend particular activities? Attendance is affected by several things including accessibility in terms of the environment, travel, how accommodating the environment is, and how affordable the activity is.

In contrast, involvement is a more complex construct, and includes elements of engagement, motivation, participation, social connection and affect. Involvement can be measured by considering 'how much' – how involved is your child actually in that activity. Are they just a passenger in the activity, or are they actively being involved and contributing to the outcome of that activity? Many a parent, regardless of whether their child has a disability or not, has brought their child to an activity and then had their child refuse to participate. A good friend of mine told me stories of how she would take her child to swimming lessons every week, but her child refused to get in the pool and participate in the swimming lesson – while that child was in attendance at the activity, and she went weekly (until her mum gave up and chose to do home swimming lessons), she was not actively engaged and participating in the activity.

When considering activities for your child to participate in, make sure you consider not only whether you are able to attend, but also (and importantly) whether your child will actively be able to and want to be involved in the activity. For this reason, it is important to choose activities that your child is interested in, and wants to participate in.

These principles of participation apply across all environments for your child – including in a therapy session, at home with the family, and out in the community with friends or peers. Your child is actively participating *only* when they are actively involved in the activity. Being actively involved requires their active participation, which is underpinned by their engagement, their motivation, their relationship with the people involved, and their mood at the time. To increase your child's active involvement, you can use a number of strategies:

- Allow your child a choice of activities that they might want to participate in. This means that your child is able to choose activities that they prefer, and can contribute to making a decision based on their own preferences and interests.

- Give your child opportunity to actively participate – ensure they are initiating movement, or at least contributing to the completion of any movement or action or activity. Doing things entirely for your child or to your child without any involvement from them is not ideal participation.

- Make sure the activities you do have a purpose, or that you set a purpose with your child for their participation in the activity. For example, the purpose for the activity might be to get out in the community to socialise with others. Or the purpose you might set for the activity with your child is to allow them to practise communicating with new people. Or the purpose might just be to have some fun and down time with your child. Setting a purpose for an activity can help your child to be much more engaged in the activity and help you to take advantage of any opportunity it offers in terms of your child's development. It also might help to set some expectations for yourself about what you want to get out of the activity, and help you and your child to not feel overwhelmed by the activity and to celebrate the success when you achieve the part of the activity you were aiming for.

- Give your child a role that contributes to the overall outcomes or achievement of the activity. At home or in a therapy setting, this might mean that your child helps to turn the pages of the book while you read, or your child passes the puzzle piece and you place it in the puzzle board. In a life setting, it might mean that your child lets everyone know when dinner is ready, or they are in charge of marking off the shopping list when you go grocery shopping or responsible for bringing their plate back to the sink when they have finished dinner. No matter how small the task or responsibility is, giving your child an active role to play in your household, your family, and within their daily life allows your child to develop a sense of accomplishment and contribution.

Passions and interests

Your child's passions and interests can be in line with their strengths, which we discussed in part II. Typically, your child's passions often become their strengths, simply because they have an interest in that area, they regularly practise that strength, and are motivated to continually improve on that strength.

As mentioned in the beginning of this chapter, passions and interests are also part of what helps your child to develop their self-identity. Let's think about the flow-on effects if your child is given the opportunity to pursue their passions and interests. Allowing your child to explore and understand their passions and interests can result in enhanced participation because they are motivated and enthusiastic about that particular activity or interest. Your child's motivation and enthusiasm will help them to continue to challenge their abilities within that area of interest. This will lead to increased mastery over the activities they are practising, and an increased sense of accomplishment and capability. Pursuing their interests and passions can also lead to building connections with other people who share their interests and passions, and participating in activities with others. This can lead to an improved sense of themselves and who they are in the world and their relationships with other people. And having an understanding of their relationships with other people, who value the things your child can contribute, again can increase their sense of self-identity and self-worth.

Allowing your child to explore their passions and interests requires you as a parent, and also others involved in your child's care, to let go of any negative beliefs associated with that area of passion or interest. Sometimes parents can be wary about allowing their child to follow their passions, especially if their child tends to have very narrow interests, and the parent would like the child to broaden their interests and horizons. This can occur for children with autism, who can have very narrow, but very significant interest and knowledge in specific topics or activities. This is absolutely understandable – you want your child to be able to be involved in a variety of life activities and situations, and variety enables your child to develop their abilities and capabilities across all areas of their development. Alternatively, parents also can worry that their child's significant passions is another difference that sets the child apart from other children their age, and that that difference may be perceived in a negative way. However, your child's strengths, passions and interests are actually a really good place to start, providing a platform from which you can then extend their interests and passions into other areas.

By harnessing your child's strengths, passions and interests, you can:

- *More easily engage your child:* Your child will more easily and happily engage with others and participate in activities that relate to their area of interest or passion. This can help your child to develop a sense of mastery, and with higher engagement levels you may be able to challenge your child to stretch their interests to other activities.

- *Help your child to work on other skills:* You can use their interest in a specific area to progress their skills in other areas, such as their ability to interact or communicate with others, their self-help or self-care skills, or their behaviour.

- *Help your child to develop a sense of themselves:* By allowing your child to pursue their strengths, passions and interests, your child learns to feel valued and accepted for who they are. In addition, your child connecting with other people who share the same passions or interests can help them to further develop their sense of self through their relationships with others and sense of social acceptance.

Every child, whether they are typically developing or have developmental delays or disabilities, will have strengths, passions or interests. Some children will naturally gravitate and take to activities involving music or dance. Some children will naturally be more adept at ball skills and team sports. Some children will naturally be better at maths than English. And, as mentioned in chapter 8, as adults, our strengths are often harnessed for the greater good for ourselves and others, within the workplace and at home. As adults, our strengths, passions and interests are celebrated and utilised, while we can still work on other activities or skills that do not come as naturally to us. The same approach should apply for your child with a disability – their natural affinity and strength for a particular type of task, activity or skill can be harnessed, while they are still working on expanding their skills in other areas.

Sports and physical activity

I've included sports and physical activity in this chapter, but maybe not entirely for the reasons you think. Fairly obviously, the benefits of sports and physical activity for your child are the same as those for any other person and child, including improved:

- mood
- behaviour
- sleep
- physical skills
- cardio-vascular fitness
- bone density
- muscle strength
- digestion.

However, sports and physical activity offer so much more benefit as a result of the participation aspect of the sports and physical activity, including the following:

- *Routine and commitment:* Regular participation in physical activity or sports provides some degree of structure and routine in your child's life. In addition, if your child plays a team sport or participates in a physical activity with a squad, your child is learning to show commitment to not only their goals, but also other people (their team mates and their coach).

- *Goal setting, persistence and resilience:* Setting goals, working towards achieving those goals, learning to cope with setbacks or losses, and continually striving to improve are all important skills to be gained that will help your child in their future life.

- *Motivation:* Participating in a physical activity or sport is so much more motivating than attending therapy sessions! Your child will learn to be internally motivated to improve and better themselves and their performance of activities, which will have a flow-on effect to their everyday abilities.

- *Teamwork:* Working with others, following the rules, turn-taking, and learning that everyone has a role to play in achieving an overall goal can be very beneficial to your child's life beyond the sporting field.
- *Friends:* Spending time with other people and sharing in an interest or passion is a great way for your child to build friendships with other like-minded people.
- *Memories and sense of identity:* Attending training, sharing in experiences with their team mates or fellow sportspeople, participating in games or competition, and working through challenges – all of these are memories that your child can have as a result of participating in a sport or physical activity that can help them to develop their sense of identity outside of their disability. They can identify themselves as a swimmer or a wheelchair basketball player, and can relate to other people on a level separate to their disability.

The following sections provide some strategies to find or create opportunities for sports or physical activity in your child's life.

Use of physical activity equipment

All children, regardless of their level of physical or cognitive disability, have the capacity to participate in physical activity. You just need to find the right activity or equipment to support their participation. Depending on your child's postural support needs, your child should be able to participate in some kind of upright physical activity using either a standing frame, a suspension gait system, or a walking frame. Great sports programs are being developed all the time for people in walking frames. Alternatively, your child might be able to use a self-propelling wheelchair for physical activity, either on their own, or as part of a team. And finally, even if your child has very severe disabilities, your child may still be able to participate in swimming or physical activity in the water or hydrotherapy. Even just being in the water can increase your child's cardiovascular levels. Moving in the water is also much easier because your child's body weight is supported, and they do not need to hold their body weight up.

Build physical activity into your child's daily routine

For example, your child might use their standing frame at school during the morning session. They then might go into their walker during the play breaks. In the afternoon, your child might complete some household chores or routine daily activities in their walker, such as collecting the mail, or putting their clothes away. You can rig up a bag or a basket that can attach to their walker or wheelchair so that they can carry the mail/their clothes, and still use their hands to get around.

Some other options include:

- Finding a friend who your child can do a sport or physical activity with.

- Joining a local sports or activity group that involves physical activity. Depending on your child's needs and abilities, the group can either be a 'mainstream' group, or a specialised sports or physical activity group.

Validating your child summary points

- Your child needs the opportunity to develop their self-identity – an understanding of who they are as a person, outside of their disability.

- You can help your child to develop a strong sense of who they are by fostering their independence, helping them to experience mastery and develop resilience.

- Presuming your child is capable, and teaching others to presume your child is capable, helps your child develop a sense of competence, self-worth and value.

- Being able to ask for help is an important skill for your child to learn that will enhance their capabilities.

- Don't forget the importance of letting your child to 'just be a kid' – to experience all the normal things that kids do, such as free play, building relationships with other people, and time and space by themselves.

- Supporting your child to pursue their passions and interests, participate in activities of their choosing, and in sports or physical activities will help them to develop their self-identity.

Part V: Empower yourself and your family

Part of your child being able to live a happy and connected life relies on them having a family, understanding who they are within that family, and having strong relationships and supports within their family. Being part of a strong supportive family also allows your child to experience a rich life.

However, family life can be stressful, even at the best of times. If you add to that situation a child with a disability, the strain experienced by the parents and family can increase. It is essential for the whole family unit to be considered when supporting children with a disability, because your child exists and functions within your family unit. If you, the parent, or other members of the family are struggling, this will affect your child. This is why I have devoted this final part of the BRAVE model and the book to the importance of empowering and supporting yourself and your family.

The benefits of having a strong and supportive family unit can be seen in numerous case examples of children I have seen over my years as a therapist. I would like to share one example with you now.

Case study

Colby is a young man who I have known since he was a boy in primary school. Colby is one of three children who grew up on a farm in our local area. Colby has cerebral palsy that affects his arms, legs and trunk. Colby requires a wheelchair to get around, and uses a picture board to communicate with the help of his family, friends and carers. Regardless of his movement or communication difficulties, Colby is a very active member of his family and his family's life, and has developed a strong personality as a result of these experiences. Colby loves being on the farm, getting into the four-wheeler buggy, getting onto the harvester and doing jobs with his Dad. Colby has been on camping and overseas holidays with his family, and his family has been very active in making sure that Colby has lead a very 'normal' life with 'normal' expectations of him as a member of the family. I think that this has led to Colby developing a very strong sense of self – indeed, Colby is very certain about what he wants and does not want in life. For a very long time, Colby refused to use any kind of power devices for either mobility or communication. His previous OT told me that when they trialled a power wheelchair with him when he was younger, he refused to touch the joystick, even though he was capable of doing so. He has always refused to trial an electronic communication device. He refuses to wear AFOs. It is only now, as a young adult, that he is interested in trialling a power wheelchair. Reading this, you might be thinking, *Gee, he sounds like a stubborn and difficult kid*, and in some respects you are right. But I think that is a reflection of his strong sense of self, and that has been fostered by his family and his place within his family. Colby sees himself as a farm boy, now a farm bloke, and technology doesn't have a place in a country boy's life. He likes things to be simple and he likes to be around his family.

We did an equipment trial with Colby, after which his parents asked him if he wanted to go home in Mum's car or in Dad's car. Colby chose Dad's ute, so his Dad helped him into the front seat and buckled him in. Seeing him sitting up there with his sunnies on, in the front seat of the ute, he looked like any other young man travelling with his Dad in the car. I was really impressed by how happy this young man was in the life he was leading.

Colby's parents have looked after themselves as well as looking after Colby and his siblings. This has allowed their family to develop a lot of resilience, to remain strong as a family, and to work together to support Colby to be the best version of himself he can be. In the chapters in this part, I take you through some of the aspects to consider so you can do the same for your family and child.

CHAPTER FOURTEEN

Working out values and making time for what's important

Having a child is a very stressful time for any couple. Having a child who has difficulties around the time of the birth, who has developmental delays, or who is diagnosed with a disability can be even more stressful. People deal with grief differently, and people parent differently – and if two parents do each of these things differently, it can extraordinarily stressful. Then add to this the additional medical and therapy appointments, and the extra meetings with schools or funding agencies, and you can understand why, sometimes, parenting a child with special needs can be a struggle.

Research has shown that parents of children with a disability report poorer levels of physical and mental health than parents of children who are typically developing. This can be related to a multitude of reasons, including that a child with a disability is likely to require more or different care than another typically developing child. Parents of children with disabilities are also likely to be dealing with additional and different stresses – such as numerous appointments, physical care requirements for their child, meetings with day care or school and support workers, navigating systems, advocating for their child, financial stressors as a result of your child's care needs and difficulty gaining or maintaining employment. These stressors are different from those originally anticipated when embarking on your parenting journey, and are potentially different from what your parents, siblings and friends have experienced or will experience with their children, which can lead to a feeling of isolation. These difficulties are real for many parents of children with developmental delays and disabilities. As a result, it is even more important that you learn, from the outset, to take care of yourself, to take care of your partner, and to take care of your other children.

Understanding your values and your family values

The reality is, there is only so much time in a day or week or month, and there is only so much one or two people (that is, you, the parents) can do with their time. Many parents of children with a disability tell me they don't have enough time in their day to do everything that needs to be done, or that they wish they had more time. The life of a parent of a child with special needs can be pretty busy and demanding. Many parents will end up needing to take their child to at least one appointment per week. They might have to physically feed their child, either by their mouth or via a PEG feeding tube. They might have to give their child medications, and complete therapy programs and onerous paperwork for funding agencies – all things that parents of typically developing children don't have to deal with. It is a definite, real issue. Time is a finite resource. We only have 24 hours in every day that we can use to do what we need to do. Unfortunately, no one can give you more time. Feeling like you don't have enough time creates added stress in your life. It makes you feel like you are not doing enough, and that you are wasting the time you do have. I can say this from experience.

When I was heavily pregnant with my son, I had an almost two and a half year old, a small business with two other part-time physios,

Working out values and making time for what's important

and was in the middle of negotiating a lease on my first commercial premises so we could open up our first clinic. Before my son was four months old, I had signed the lease, organised a builder for the fit out, ordered the furniture, put the furniture together (argh, flat packs!), organised signage and employed my first admin officer. This was a crazy time in my life. In the following months, I also started to return to work, mostly working behind the scenes, with only a minimal amount of hands-on work as a therapist. During this time I was really struggling with feeling like my work was taking over my life. The whole reason I started my business was to be around for when my kids were little, to spend time with them, and to be able to work school hours when they started school. I was feeling like work was encroaching on that vision, and I didn't feel like I was doing 'the right thing' by my kids. I was cranky and stressed, and this affected my time with them and my husband. I knew something had to change.

It was at this stage that I met a physio business mentor, and I did a course he was running. During this course, he got us to do an exercise to identify our personal values – the things we think are really important to us, and we place high priority on. Values are the big picture things in our lives that we 'live for', the things we wake up for every morning. Doing the exercise, I identified that my family was my number one priority, which was not a huge surprise. However, the outcome of identifying my values was that I was able to start making conscious decisions about my life that were in line with my values, instead of in contrast with my values. It helped me to start prioritising my family, and making decisions about my work, my business and my role that was in line with putting my family first. And knowing my values helped me to make decisions with more confidence, and without so much guilt. In addition, it helped me to better understand how I wanted to use my time. As a result, I was able to use my time more effectively on the tasks that mattered, rather than on everything. I wasn't able to find more time or to make more time, I just learnt to use my time more effectively on the things I wanted to focus on and which were in alignment with my values. This has considerably decreased my stress levels and my feelings of not doing enough or not being a good enough parent.

As a parent who has a multitude of areas in which you need to spend your time, this exercise might also prove useful for you. And remember – everyone's values are different. By doing this exercise, you can identify what is important to you, and use that to make decisions in line with your own values, not what anyone else has experienced or thinks. It also allows you to decide what really matters in your life, and make decisions that are in line with that.

Working out what your personal values are is the first step, and you can use numerous online tools to explore and figure out what your personal values might be. Some of these tools simply provide a list of values from which you can select the ones that feel the most important to you. Alternatively, other tools take you through a series of questions exploring different aspects of your life, your thinking and your goals to determine what your values are. This process is useful if you are feeling a bit lost and not sure where to start. Regardless of which strategy you use, even just being aware of the things you highly value or consider important in your life can help you to start making decisions in line with those values.

Once you are familiar with your personal values, you can then start to make decisions based on those values. For example, if family is one of your personal values, when considering therapies or treatments for your child, you might want to consider the impact of those therapies or treatments on the rest of your family and how your family spends time together. You might decide that during the week you will focus on your child's development, and weekends and school holidays are times to focus on making memories as a family.

If one of your personal values is your career or your profession, you might make a decision to return to work casually or part-time to help you fulfil that value. If one of your values is connection with a community, you might take steps to find a group of other parents you can connect with or you might look for activities that will allow you to meet with other families similar to your own. Or if one of your values is to give back to others, you might reach out to other parents to provide support or develop a support group or charity to help other people within your community.

A very helpful extension to the exercise is to also get your partner to identify their values. Again, everyone's personal values are different, so your partner's values might differ to yours (and you might not realise this). My husband and I each did our personal values, and then we came together to discuss our personal values and come up with some values that we would like for us as a family. This has helped to keep both of our visions in alignment, and to make sure we are each working towards a similar path for our children and family.

Taking the time you and your family need

Learning to look after your child with a disability, and learning to fit your child's needs into a life that suits you and your family does not happen overnight. It can take a while to 'find your feet' and get into a rhythm of managing your child's and family's needs … and then it can all be upheaved when a change or a problem comes up. It is important that, during this process of learning, you are kind to yourself, kind to each other, and you give yourself time to learn to manage the best you can.

Taking time for yourself and your partner

Making sure you look after yourself so that you can look after your child or children is something often shared within new parent magazines, websites, Facebook pages (and more), but the message is even more important for you as the parent of a child with disabilities, who has to spend so much more time caring for your child, and over a more prolonged period of time. Looking after yourself enables you to have the energy and mental space to be able to devote time to your child and deal with any challenges that come your way. Burnout is a thing, and you want to avoid emotional fatigue, empathy fatigue and vicarious trauma. You can help do so by making sure you look after yourself and take time for yourself.

What can you do to look after yourself? Have time away from your child or children. Follow your own interests outside of your child and children. Take time to have a break. This can be a five-minute cup of tea while your child is resting, or a morning out of the house or a weekend away with your friends. Taking a break can help you to think clearly about any challenges you have been worrying about.

I remember when my son was about four or five months old and he would not sleep – okay, I lie. He would sleep if we were holding him, but he would not sleep in his bassinet. I was at my wits' end, and had had enough. I knew I needed a break, I needed a time out. So I told my husband I was going to go out for an hour or two, and I left him at home with the kids. During that time I went to the beach (a five-minute drive from our house), read through a baby sleep guide and stopped at McDonald's for a cup of hot chocolate and a muffin. Nothing amazing or glamourous. But being away from the house and the situation that was so stressful for me allowed me the opportunity to think clearly about what was happening with my son's sleeping, and to come up with a plan about what to do about it.

And how can you find time for your partner? Go for a walk together. Go out on a date night (or a date lunch or coffee if escaping the house for dinner is too hard). Spend some time each night, with the phones, TVs and iPads off, connecting with each other by just chatting and discussing any challenges so you can address them together. Give your partner a hug (for at least 20 seconds – research shows that you need to hug for 20 seconds to allow the release of endorphins). Show your partner that you are grateful for them and how they might have helped you out that day. Ask questions and explore what each other thinks and feels about different situations, and really listen to what they are saying. And make sure you talk about things other than your children and your child with special needs.

Working out values and making time for what's important

Taking time for your other children

In among the crazy busyness that is your life trying to look after your child with special needs, you also need to consider taking time for and spending time with your other children. Your other children will realise that their sibling with special needs requires more of your time and attention for their daily needs. And having a sibling with special needs will have some significant benefits for your other children – they will develop empathy and acceptance of others, and they are likely to become more responsible and resilient. However, it is important to make sure your other children feel equally as loved and valued within your family unit.

Taking time for your other children not only helps them to feel important and special, but also helps your child with a disability to understand the world and your family doesn't revolve around them. Taking time for your other children involves both spending focused time with your other children, either together (if you have more than one sibling) or individually, as well as treating all your children similarly, and not giving your child with a disability special treatment beyond what is necessary, such as still giving your child with a disability jobs and responsibilities around the house (as appropriate for their abilities), and making sure all children have the same expectations for completing these jobs and responsibilities. This will have positive effects for both your child with special needs and their siblings.

Some practical ways you can take time for your other children include the following:

- Spend time with your other children on their own, in one-on-one situations, doing activities of their choice that they enjoy.

- Make sure your other children still get to pursue their own passions and interests. So if your other child plays soccer, their soccer games should continue to be considered as important, with family activities also arranged around these important events.

- Tell your other children what is happening for their sibling with special needs.

- Involve your other children in their sibling's care, but only to the level that they want to (you don't want caring for their sibling to become a burden).

- Make sure your other children's successes, as well as their contributions to the family, are recognised, celebrated and valued. Sometimes the achievements of your other children, and their efforts and the assistance they provide to help out around the house or with their sibling can be overlooked or taken for granted, because the needs and achievements of the sibling with special needs can seem so important. Your other children need to be celebrated in the same way as their sibling with special needs, and to be valued for their efforts and contributions.

Fitting your child's needs into a life you choose

Parents of children with special needs can easily get caught up in trying to do everything they can to assist their child to be the best they can be. A result of this is that everything for the child with special needs is prioritised over everything else in life. As you can imagine, this can have detrimental effects on the whole family's wellbeing and satisfaction with life.

Before you had children, or before your child was diagnosed with a disability, I am sure there were things in your life and your family's life that held importance, or that you valued. This might have been having a family holiday every year, or spending Sunday dinners with the extended family, or having some down time before bed together as a family each night. It is important that these life habits or rhythms are maintained as much as possible so that the life you lead raising your child with special needs is in line with the life you had envisaged for yourself, or a life that you feel satisfied with.

Understanding your values, and making decisions about your child's and family's life that are in line with those values is one strategy you can use to make sure your child's needs still fit within the life and lifestyle that gives you a sense of satisfaction and connection. Some further strategies to help you to feel like your child's needs are fitting into a life you choose include the following:

- *Continue with important family rituals or habits:* My family ritual is to have dinner together with all our immediate family members each night whenever possible. Work out what your important family rituals or habits are and try to organise your child's routines around them. Make sure your therapists also understand the importance of certain family rituals or habits so that they can develop programs or routines or schedules that will assist you to maintain these.

- *Build your child's therapy into their daily life routine:* Instead of trying to add therapy on to your child's everyday activities, think of ways you can incorporate developmental activities into their daily life. This might mean doing an exercise every morning before putting their shoes on, or practising a thinking activity while brushing their teeth. Doing this will decrease the feeling of having to squeeze additional tasks and activities into the day.

- *Continue to do family activities as a family:* Some activities you used to do as a family might be a bit more difficult, but activities can be adapted in many ways to help your child with special needs to participate. Talk with your child's therapists for tips on how you can adapt specific family activities so your child with a disability can participate, or discuss with them alternative activities you might be able to do as a family.

Safe manual handling

As a physiotherapist, I could not write this section without making sure I included information about safe manual handling for parents and other members of the family.

Manual handling relates to the way we handle objects in our lives. As a parent of a child with a disability, you may need to support your child's physical movements and provide physical care to your child well after we are typically expected to as parents. In addition, you may need to handle different pieces of equipment, such as wheelchairs, hoists, walking frames and shower chairs. Any task that involves you pushing, pulling, lifting, sliding, or moving your child or any of the equipment involved in their care should ideally be done with a safe technique to ensure you are able to continue caring for your child, and that your own body remains in good health and working order.

When transferring your child or helping them to move, the best way you can help to decrease your own load and strain is to get your child to do as much as they possibly can for themselves. Whenever you are supporting your child to move, consider the parts of the transfer your child can help with. Anything your child can do to help will decrease the load that you have to manage. Your child's therapists can also work with you and your child to figure out how your child can assist with any transfer so the manual handling load on you is decreased.

You can get further help on how to manage your child's physical needs safely from your child's therapists or care providers. Your child's therapists can demonstrate safe lifting techniques that are specific to your child's needs, and how to use the equipment for your child safely. You can also ask your child's therapists to prepare manual handling plans or transfer procedures – these are documents that outline the correct handling and transfer procedures for specific activities in your child's daily life. These types of plans are useful for when other members of the family or friends are available or come to help you with your child's care, or if you are away and another person needs to help your child with their transfers.

Safe manual handling also relies on you keeping your body as strong, healthy and flexible as needed to manage the physical tasks you need to do, and you listening to your body when it is letting you know you need to rest or some extra help. Staying fit and strong will always assist to keep you safe when helping to move or transfer or care for your child. Being aware of your body positions and movements, and how frequently you do them throughout the day, can help you to identify movements or transfers that are more risky than others. And listening to your body when it is fatigued, tired, strained or feeling weak will allow you to adapt your transfer or care strategy so as to not compromise your own safety when moving or caring for your child.

Managing the mental load

The challenge of managing the mental load as a parent has been talked about at length through research and through general media. However, raising a child with a disability and helping them to live their best life does come with an additional mental load. Attending specialist and therapy appointments, researching your child's condition and treatment or therapy approaches, filling in paperwork for funding or enrolment into programs or services, knowing when your child's care meetings are coming up and what information you need to gather prior to attending, knowing what medications your child needs when and remembering when their doses change – the list of additional tasks that you have to remember, prepare for, and make decisions about is not insubstantial. Add to that the worry about your child's wellbeing and whether you are doing enough for your child, along with the guilt you might feel if you forget something or if feel like you just need to take a break from this load for your own mental health, and it is understandable that many parents I meet have felt overwhelmed with having to coordinate everything related to their child's care.

While it may not be possible to remove or decrease the mental load, my focus for this section is to share some strategies that might help you to manage the mental load without feeling overwhelmed. These strategies are:
- *Incorporating self-care:* The importance of self-care and how to build self-care into your life has been covered earlier in this

chapter. However, I want to reiterate that taking time out for yourself can help you to feel more refreshed and revived, enabling you to be more ready and better able to manage the ongoing needs of your child and family. Remember, raising children is a marathon, not a sprint. You need to be able to look out for yourself to last the distance.

- *Planning your day/week/month:* Having a diary, weekly schedule, or wall calendar in a central part of your household can help with taking the information you need to remember out of your head – and so help to remove the load from your mind. You could have a whiteboard with the days of the week listed, and each member of the family can schedule in their activities for the week or month or year. At my house, we have a year calendar where we write down the big events we need to be prepared for, and then a weekly planner where we write down each person's activities for the week. Planning your day, week or month in advance can help you, your partner, and your family prepare and plan ahead, such as deciding ahead of time who will take each child to their respective appointments or activities.

- *Scheduling time-out or self-care time:* When putting things down on a weekly or monthly schedule, you also have a great opportunity to schedule in self-care time or family time, to ensure you maintain a balance in your lives. You can look for gaps in your activities where you can plan for fun or restorative activities – or, even better, you can schedule the fun or restorative activities in first, before booking anything else in. While it is one thing to schedule these activities in, it is another to honour that schedule and actually go through with doing these activities. The everyday tasks and appointments or other activities for your child can easily creep into the times when you would otherwise be taking time out as a family or individually. This is where remembering and considering your values (discussed earlier in this chapter) comes in handy.

- *Choosing to say 'no' to activities or opportunities if the mental or physical load will outweigh the benefits for your child or family:* It can be tempting to say 'yes' to every opportunity available for your child with a disability, because you want to give them every chance to develop as much as they can. However, not all opportunities are equal, and sometimes the gain to be made will not outweigh the extra effort you or your child will have to make to attend or participate in the opportunity. For example, if your child participates in a physical activity program that leaves them so fatigued that they cannot participate at school or their behaviour is affected, participation in that program might not be worth it. Alternatively, participation in an activity might mean your other children miss out on their activities, or might take you away from your family for long periods of time. As a family you need to consider your values, and decide if these negative consequences are worth it for the potential gains.
- *Seeking help when you need it:* Sometimes the mental load of any parent can get too much. It is important to feel comfortable enough to be able to reach out to other people for help when you need it. Strategies to find the help and support you need are covered in the next chapter.

CHAPTER FIFTEEN

Finding support and choosing your battles

An important aspect of looking after yourself is reaching out for help when you need it. However, if you are anything like me, and many other parents, you might be quite stoic, and reaching out for help may not come naturally. I think this comes from our current times – we often live further away from our families and the communities we grew up in, and we are taught to be independent and can be independent from very early in life. And although our access to technology means we have lots of methods for connection – including Facebook, Instagram, Messenger, instant messaging and emails – we are actually often more disconnected from others than ever. Back in 'the olden days' the saying was 'it takes a village to raise a child', but in our efforts to be independent, self-sufficient and connected primarily via technology, we seem to have lost this approach. However, you can take steps to try to connect with others whom you can call upon for help. This is what can be described as finding your tribe, and I discuss this idea in this chapter, along with the importance of advocating for your child – and knowing when to focus on other battles.

Finding your tribe

Your tribe are the people you can call upon when you need help, advice or support, have some questions, or need to cry with someone and commiserate or whinge. They are also the people who you can reciprocate this with – being able to provide advice to others boosts our self-confidence and boosts our sense of worth and value.

Who might your tribe consist of?

The members of your tribe could include the following:

- *Your partner:* Your partner will hopefully be one of the most important people in your tribe. Through following the strategies discussed in the preceding chapter, hopefully you and your partner will be able to work together to meet the needs of your child and family, and can provide a strong support for each other.

- *Other parents:* This might be parents in your local community or parents from afar but who share the same experiences as you. You can meet these people through local parent groups and workshops you attend, by waiting in the waiting area with them, or online through platforms like Facebook groups. Finding other parents in similar circumstances to you can help you to feel less alone in times of difficulty or stress, and to feel connected with other people who understand what it is you are going through.

- *Health professionals:* This might include doctors, specialists, therapists or practice nurses involved in your child's care. Look for health professionals who support both you and your child, help you to feel knowledgeable and empowered about your child's care, and who you can call on for help when you need it.

- *Teachers or carers from the school or community:* Again, look for teachers and carers who can help you to support your child, and whom you can call upon for help when you need it.
- *Other advocates in the community:* This might include community groups for children with your child's diagnosis or generally for special needs, neighbourhood support groups, or even your local parliamentary member. These advocates could be local to your area, but given the reach you can get from the internet and social media these days, you could potentially also find supports and advocates from other areas across the world.

How do you find your tribe?

Not everyone is going to be the right fit for you and your tribe. A bit like when making friends, your tribe is going to consist of people who you can get along with, who have a similar attitude and outlook to you, and whom you can trust. Try the following to find the right people for your tribe:

- Search for people or organisations whose values and approach feel right for your child and family.
- Search for other parents whose experiences might be similar to your own. It might be that their child has the same diagnosis as your child or similar difficulties to your child, or it might be that they live in the same area as you.
- Spend some time getting to know the people or organisations who could possibly help you with your child, and developing your and your child's trust in them.
- Look for events or activities where you might be able to meet other parents or representatives of organisations who can help you or your child. Meeting people in an informal way at community events, fundraisers, get-togethers or awareness events is a good way to get a feel for someone or an organisation before meeting with them in a more direct way such as an appointment or a one-to-one catch up.

- Don't underestimate the value of introducing yourself to other parents or families in the waiting room of your child's paediatrician or therapy service. I know of many, many parents who have learnt things and developed support networks and friendships with other parents who were also waiting in the waiting room of their local doctor, hospital, or even our clinic.

- Be sure to offer help, as well as to seek out the help of others. As a parent of a child with special needs, you have a wealth of knowledge and information that will be of benefit to other parents. You might not feel like you have a lot to offer at the beginning but, over time and as you 'find your feet', you will know a lot about many things that I, as a therapist, could not tell a parent because I don't have a child with a disability so have not lived some of the experiences you have. You can offer help to other parents in many ways – through face-to-face meetings, online chat groups or Facebook groups, and through responding to questionnaires or surveys about your experiences as a parent of a child with a disability. By sharing your experiences and knowledge, you can help another parent who is going through the same as you, and ultimately contribute to the overall support available for parents of children with disabilities.

Advocating for your child

Advocating for your child is an inevitable thing you will need to do, regardless of whether your child has a disability or not. Parents are the primary advocates for their children, when their children cannot yet advocate for themselves. Some parents of children with disabilities, however, will need to advocate more or for longer, to ensure their child can become the best they can be.

Advocating for your child relies upon you knowing your child well, and recognising what they need. Understanding your child's needs can allow you to ensure they are supported to be the best they can be, but also ensures that you don't lose sleep or energy advocating for things they don't need or that are not important.

For many parents, advocating for their child's needs will also involve listening to your child's wishes, respecting their wishes and letting them learn to speak for themselves. This is especially important as your child gets older, and starts to have more of a say in their own cares and life. This can be a difficult time in a family's life, because many times what the child wants is in contrast to what the parents would like for their child. Nevertheless, for your child to develop into a confident, happy and connected adult, they do need to be informed about the decisions they need to make, learn to make or contribute to decisions for themselves, and live with the consequences of those decisions. This is all a part of growing up.

Your ability to advocate for your child also relies on your knowledge of how you can help, and/or where you can go to get further help if you need it. It is important to understand your own strengths and weaknesses in relation to advocating for your child, and seek the help of others if you are feeling stretched or overwhelmed. In addition, it is important to ask questions to ensure you know all the details about your child's needs, all the options available to meet those needs, who you can approach to get the help you need, and the process to escalate your concerns if you are feeling unhappy or dissatisfied with what is happening for your child. Being as informed and knowledgeable as possible will help you to approach advocating for your child with confidence and conviction.

Simply by reading this book and spending time getting to know your child and their needs will help you to become a better advocate for your child. Some other strategies that can help you to more effectively advocate for your child include:

- *Maintain positive relationships with the people involved in your child's care:* Having positive, open lines of communication and trusting relationships with your child's health professionals, therapists, teachers or carers can help you to feel more comfortable when bringing up any issues, and will help to ensure that you all focus on finding solutions for the difficulties or problems you would like addressed.

- *Ask questions:* Don't be afraid to ask questions. Information in the field of medicine, therapies and disability is constantly being updated, and it can be hard to stay abreast of all the available information. Your child's health professionals are expected to stay up to date, so they are a good resource to ask questions if you are not sure about something related to your child's care. Your child's health professional will be able to share with you what information is known from the most recent research, but will also be able to share with you their opinion based on their experiences with other children they work with. Another great resource of information is other parents, who can give you information about their or their child's personal experiences with a specific condition or treatment.

- *Remain calm:* When you are feeling emotional – whether it be angry, fearful, or sad – it can be hard to clearly articulate your concerns and what you would like to see improve. In addition, if the person you are talking to is feeling threatened or anxious (for example, if you are angry and yelling), it can be hard for them to take on board all that you are saying and come up with ways to address your concerns. Instead, try to remain calm when raising issues or problems. To do this you might need to give yourself time to calm down and think about how you want to bring up the problem, and you might want to write down your concerns and what response you would like to see (because the act of writing things down can help you to better understand your concerns yourself, and you can then explain these concerns more clearly to the other person).

- *If necessary, put concerns in writing, and ask for responses in writing:* This will help you to more clearly articulate your concerns (as mentioned in the preceding point), but will also help you to keep a record of the steps you have taken to try to have the issue addressed, and the response you have been given at each stage.

- *Be persistent, and understand the pathways available for escalating your concerns:* If you are not getting a response, or you are not getting the result you want, it is important to continue to advocate and know which steps you need to take to escalate your concerns. Each person or provider you and your child work with should have a process for escalating concerns – follow that process, keep a record of each step and the response given so that you can refer back to it as needed.

- *Get someone to help you:* Persistently advocating for your child can be a tiring process. Getting someone to help you can not only decrease the load on you, but also can provide you with an ally during meetings or difficult discussions. This person can also listen and take notes to help you remember everything.

- *Know when to let it go:* Whether it be because you have exhausted your avenues for advocacy, whether the costs have started to outweigh the benefits, or the fight just does not seem worth it, it is important to know when to choose to 'let it go'.

Choosing your battles

Unfortunately, frequent, stressful or continuous advocating for your child's needs can be taxing on you as a parent, as well as on your family. When advocating for your child's needs, it is important to continue to look after yourself, and to recognise when the advocating is coming at the detriment of your, your child's or your family's overall wellbeing. As a result, it is important to be able to decide when you are going to advocate for your child, and when you are going to consciously choose not to advocate for your child.

Just like anyone else, not every battle you come across is going to be worth it, and you might find yourself in a situation where choosing to fight and the gain to be made for your child is just not worth the required physical or mental effort to achieve it. To keep your perspective on whether the battle is worth it, try to keep the end in mind – will this problem matter in five or 10 years' time? Will this problem be a big issue when your child is an adult? Is the issue and the effort and sacrifices you will have to make in line with your personal or family values? And are you acting on principle only rather than for a specific benefit for your child?

No-one will be able to make a decision for you about whether or not to fight each battle you are facing. But being as informed as possible and understanding what is important to you and your child will help you to make a decision that is right for your individual circumstances. I also want to reiterate – choosing not to fight a battle is not a sign of weakness or failure. In my mind, it is actually a sign of courage and strength, because you are able to recognise what is most important in your child's and family's life, accept a sacrifice of sorts, and choose to take a better path.

In the previous chapter, I outlined that there are only so many hours in a day, week or month. In addition, your child is only a child for a short amount of time in the whole scheme of things. It is important that you spend the time you have to help your child as wisely as possible. And, sometimes, that will mean letting go of battles that are not important, and focusing on what is.

Empowering yourself and your family summary points

- Your child exists within the context of your family. You, the parent, and the rest of the family also need to be supported to ensure the best outcomes for your child.

- Helping your child with a disability be the best they can be is a marathon, not a sprint. You need to look after yourself both physically and mentally. If you are not feeling your best, it is much harder for you to then help your child.

- Understanding your personal and family values can help to guide your decisions in relation to your child's care.

- Time out on your own, with your partner, with your other children, and also to just have fun with your child with a disability, will help you to manage in the long term.

- Try to fit your child's needs into a life you choose, not the other way around.

- Reaching out for help will be necessary at times. Build your own tribe of people who you can call upon when needed.

CONCLUSION

Bringing it all together

All parents, regardless of whether our children have a disability or not, have the same hopes for our children – for them to be happy, healthy, confident, connected and fulfilled. While this wish might seem like a reasonable ask for parents whose child is typically developing (even though the journey can certainly have some difficulties), it can sometimes seem very distant or out of reach for parents of children with developmental delays or disabilities. When you realise or find out your child has a developmental delay or disability, your trajectory of how your child might develop and grow up is changed, and it can leave you feeling lost and unsure of the next steps. And while all parents enter their parenting journey not really knowing how they are supposed to give their child the best life they can, hundreds (and maybe even thousands!) of books for parents of typically developing children can help them to navigate this journey (and I have a small library of these on my own bookshelves at home). In addition, parents of typically developing children can call upon their own parents, other family members or friends to ask of their experiences and to help them navigate some of the usual difficulties because they have dealt with that issue themselves. However, in comparison, hardly any books are available for parents of children with disabilities, and your own parents or friends might not be such a good resource for information.

My hope is that, after reading this book, you now feel empowered with knowledge that will help you to help your child to be the best they can be:

- You are aware of the possible signs of developmental delay or disability, and you can confidently seek out help for your concerns as early as possible.

- You understand the importance of seeking help and support for your child's development as early as possible in order to maximise the opportunities for improvement for your child.

- You have an understanding of the breadth of your child's needs, how each of those areas of need are interconnected, and strategies to now identify and prioritise your child's needs across all areas of development.

- You know how to support your child to develop their independence as much as possible, and why this is important.

- You understand how to help your child to develop their self-identity and self-esteem.

- You understand the importance of looking after yourself, your partner, and your other children, and fitting your child's needs into the rest of your family's life.

The BRAVE model upon which this book is based is designed to take you right from the beginning of your journey, from being aware of the early signs of childhood developmental delay or disability, right through to the stage when you are supporting your child to live independently within the community, out from under your own roof and care. The BRAVE model is something I hope you can draw from and use to organise your thoughts throughout your child's childhood, as your child develops, grows, changes and hopefully thrives.

Bringing it all together

The BRAVE model is also designed to help you think more broadly about your child's needs – beyond the usual medical needs and developmental needs, to also considering their need to develop independence and understand who they are in the world, and how they can contribute and the value they can offer to others. Ultimately, it is these broader concepts that can help your child to become connected, confident, happy and fulfilled themselves.

Importantly, however, you, as a parent, also need to be able to look after yourself in this journey of helping your child with a developmental delay or disability. Without being able to look after yourself, your ability to help your child will be compromised by fatigue, emotional exhaustion, frustration or overwhelm.

Entering into the journey of parenting a child with a developmental delay or disability can be overwhelming. You have so much information to learn, so many decisions to make, and so much that is unknown. This can make it difficult to feel confident, empowered and ready to take on the challenge. It astounded me when researching and planning for this book that not only were merely a handful of books available for parents of children with disabilities, but also that hundreds of books were available for health professionals, therapists or teachers who work with children with developmental delays and disabilities. I feel we have had the distribution of knowledge about helping children with disabilities a bit round the wrong way. I hope with this book I can contribute to adjusting the balance back a little way towards educating and empowering you, the parents.

As the parent of your child, you are the person who is going to have the most impact on your child's development, on their opportunities for improvement and progress, and on their ability to develop an understanding of who they are and what they have to contribute to this world – not your child's doctors, therapists or teachers (although they do have a role to play). You are the person who your child spends most time with and builds the closest relationship with, and it is you who will advocate most for your child. It seems fitting, then, that you should have as much knowledge as possible within your toolbox to help your child.

Where you go from here will depend on which stage you are at, and which stage your child is at. You could, for example:

- *Seek out the help of others:* You could find a health professional to answer your concerns, or to provide you with guidance on how to help your child. Or you could find the help of some parents, for problem-solving, information-sharing, or reassurance, support and friendship.

- *Review the BRAVE model:* You can work through the model again to identify which area of the model you have been missing or neglecting recently, and focus on that area. For example, if helping your child pursue their passions or looking after yourself has been neglected recently, you can take steps to focus on that to ensure the broader needs of your child and family are met.

- *Choose just one strategy from one of the sections to implement for a week or month:* Of the many specific strategies, which one do you think will help most for your child? Which one do you think feels the most important for your child? Or which one will be the easiest to implement? Any of the strategies may be useful, so it is up to you to decide which one.

No matter the stage you and your child are at, remember this: every child is unique. Every family is unique. What works for one child or family may not work for another. And your child's needs will change over time – as they grow and develop, and also as your family's needs change. So, what works for you in one stage of childhood might not also work in another stage. It is up to you to decide what is important for your child and family, and what works for your child and family, both now and into the future. However, armed with the information within this book and using the BRAVE model to guide you, I hope you now feel more confident about going forth and helping your child. And I hope you realise that you are now in a powerful position to be able to help your child be the best they can be.

Further reading and helpful resources

References

The following articles and books resources were referenced within the pages of this book:

Gladwell, M. (1963). *Outliers: the story of success.* New York: Little, Brown and Co.

Papile, L., Munsick-Bruno, G., & Schaefer, A. (1978). 'Relationship of cerebral intraventricular hemorrage and childhood neurological handicaps'. *The Journal of Pediatrics*, 103(2): 273–277. doi: https://doi.org/10.1016/S0022-3476(83)80366-7.

Poon, K. K., Watson, L. R., Baranek, G. T. & Poe, M. D. (2013). 'Research Brief: To what extent do joint attention, imitation, and object play behaviors in infancy predict later communication and intellectual functioning in ASD?' Downloaded online on February 17, 2015 at http://www.med.unc.edu/ahs/ocsci/sep/sep-image-and-files/parent-briefs/briefs-added-1-16-13/Brief_JAImitationObjectPlay_PredictCom_1-16-13.pdf.

Rosenbaum, P., Walker, S., Hanna, S., Palisano, R., Russell, D., Raina, P., Wood, E., Bartlett, D. & Galuppi, B. (2002). 'Prognosis for gross motor function in cerebral palsy: creating of motor development curves'. *JAMA*, 288 (11): 1357–1363. doi: 10.1001/jama.288.11.1357.

Sterling, C., Taub, E., Davis, D., Rickards, T., Gauthier, L., Griffin, A. & Uswatte, G. (2013). 'Structural neuroplastic change after constraint-induced movement therapy in children with cerebral palsy'. *Pediatrics*, 131(5): 2012–2051. doi: 10.1542/peds.2012-2051.

Helpful resources

The following lists additional resources in specific areas. Note that all resources lists are aimed at a general rather than academic market and are accessible for the everyday reader.

Neuroplasticity

If you'd like to read more about neuroplasticity, these books are a great place to start:

Doidge, N. (2010). *The brain that changes itself: stories of personal triumph from the frontiers of brain science.* Viking Publishers.

Pape, K. (2016). *The boy who could run but not walk: understanding neuroplasticity in the child's brain.* Barlow Books.

Personal experiences

If you'd like to read more about parents' experiences of raising their child with a disability, or the experiences of people with a disability, these books are very good reads:

Alcott, D. (2018). *Able: gold medals, grand slams and smashing glass ceilings.* Harper Collins Publishers.

Anner, Z. (2016). *If at birth you don't succeed: my adventures with disaster and destiny.* Henry Holt and Company.

Brown, I. (2009). *The boy in the moon: a father's search for his disabled son.* Random House Canada.

Koenig, C. (2008). *Paper cranes: a mother's story of hope, courage and determination.* Exisle Publishing.

Appendices

Appendix A: Common diagnoses **261**
Appendix B: Developmental milestones for children with Down syndrome **265**
Appendix C: Medical service providers **269**
Appendix D: Funding options while accessing treatment **277**

Appendix A: Common diagnoses

Provided here is a list of common diagnoses seen in children who have developmental difficulties. Literally hundreds of other rarer genetic conditions cause developmental difficulties in children; unfortunately, I could not include all of these, so I have just included a selection of the most common diagnoses.

Acquired brain injury

Brain injury that occurs in a child over approximately 12 months of age. The subsequent difficulties as a result of a brain injury can vary significantly from mild difficulties with aspects such as memory, concentration and thinking skills, to significant and severe disability.

Autism spectrum disorder (ASD)

A developmental condition in which children have difficulties in how they relate to people and things in their environment. Some of the difficulties children with ASD experience include forming and maintaining social and emotional connections and relationships with others, understanding and using nonverbal communication behaviours, and restricted or repetitive patterns of behaviour, interests or activities. The way ASD presents in different children can vary significantly (hence the use of the word 'spectrum'). Some children can have mild difficulties, and some children can have more significant or severe difficulties.

Cerebral palsy

An umbrella term describing a group of permanent disorders affecting the development of movement and posture that occur as a result of a non-progressive insult to the developing brain (that is, typically occurring before birth or during infancy). The motor difficulties in cerebral palsy are often accompanied by other associated issues such as difficulties with sensation, perception, cognition, communication, and behaviour, and by secondary musculoskeletal problems. Cerebral palsy is diagnosed in three main types:

- *Hemiplegia or unilateral:* Affects the arm and leg on one side of the body.

- *Diplegia:* Affects both sides of the body, but primarily affects the legs. The arms are minimally affected, and upper limb function often appears to be reasonably in line with typically developing peers.

- *Quadriplegia:* Affects both sides of the body, and usually affects both the arms and legs. The presentation can be (and often is) asymmetrical, so one side of the body might be affected more than the other, or it can be a combination where one arm is worse than the other and the opposite leg is worse than the other.

Down syndrome

A genetic condition that causes a number of differences including facial and limb features, and frequently cognitive impairments (although the level of cognitive impairment can be very variable). Children with Down syndrome have hypermobility (flexibility of their joints and muscles) and low tone (low resting muscle activity), which means their achievement of developmental milestones is often later than their typically developing peers. Most children with Down syndrome learn to communicate effectively, but the method they use to communicate can vary.

Global developmental delay

A general term used to describe a child with developmental delays in many areas (for example, gross motor, fine motor, communication and cognitive). Usually children with global developmental delay are considered to have lower intellectual functioning that other children their age. In my experience, the diagnosis of global developmental delay is sometimes given when no genetic cause for the child's global difficulties can be identified.

Microcephaly

A term used to describe when a baby's or child's head is abnormally small, which is usually associated with impaired growth of the brain. Some babies are born with microcephaly (congenital), and some babies develop it after birth (acquired). Some babies or children with microcephaly can develop typically because their underlying brain tissue is 'normal'. Others, as a result of the underlying impaired brain growth and development, will experience developmental consequences of that impaired brain growth.

Muscular dystrophies

A genetic condition that causes progressive weakening and wasting of the muscles of the body. The severity of weakening, the muscles affected, the age when symptoms first begin, how fast the weakening progresses, and the prognosis all vary significantly between different types of muscular dystrophy, and also between people.

Rett syndrome

A genetic brain disorder that affects girls. Most girls with Rett syndrome develop normally until 6 to 18 months of age, after which they either stop acquiring new skills or start to lose skills. Rett syndrome causes difficulties with language, coordination, movement and independence. The prognosis for girls with Rett syndrome can vary significantly.

Spina bifida

A birth defect where the spinal bones do not develop fully in utero, resulting in the spinal cord and the membranes around the spinal cord remaining exposed. Three types of spina bifida are possible, with different levels of impact:

- *Spina bifida occulta:* Occurs when the outer part of some of the vertebrae (back bone) is not completely closed, but the spinal cord and the membranes around it remain intact where they are supposed to be. Many children and adults with this type of spina bifida have no symptoms.
- *Meningocele:* Occurs when the membranes around the spinal cord push through the gap in the back bone creating a fluid-filled sac. Children with this type of spina bifida can have variable problems, depending on whether the nerves around the spinal cord are damaged.
- *Myelomeningocele:* This is the most severe form of spina bifida, where both the meninges and the spinal cord push through the gap in the back bone. Children with this type of spina bifida usually have some degree of muscle paralysis and sensory deficits due to the damage to the spinal cord and nerves around the spine.

The difficulties children with spina bifida face can vary greatly depending on the type of lesion and the severity of the nerve damage.

Appendix B: Developmental milestones for children with Down syndrome

The milestones listed in the following table have been adapted from the UK's Personal Child Health Record Book insert for babies born with Down syndrome, developed by Down Syndrome Medical Interest Group. The full insert is available at www.healthforallchildren.com/wp-content/uploads/2013/04/A5-Downs-Instrucs-chartsfull-copy.pdf.

As mentioned in chapter 3, the age ranges listed in the table are a guide only; your child might achieve these motor milestones earlier or later than the age ranges listed.

Milestone	Average age (and range) for children with Down syndrome	Average age (and range) for typically developing children
Gross motor		
Holds head steady when sitting	5 months (3–5 months)	3 months (1–4 months)
Rolls over	8 months (4–12 months)	5 months (2–10 months)
Sits alone	9 months (6–30 months)	7 months (5–9 months)
Stands alone	18 months (12–38 months)	11 months (9–16 months)
Walks alone	23 months (13–48 months)	12 months (9–18 months)

Milestone	Average age (and range) for children with Down syndrome	Average age (and range) for typically developing children
Fine motor		
Follows object with eyes	3 months (1.5–6 months)	1.5 months (1–3 months)
Reaches out and grasps objects	6 months (4–11 months)	4 months (2–6 months)
Passes objects hand to hand	8 months (6–12 months)	5.5 months (4–8 months)
Builds a tower of two cubes	30 months (14–32 months)	15 months (10–19 months)
Copies a circle	48 months (36–60 months)	30 months (24–40 months)
Language		
Responds to sounds	1 month (0.5–1.5 months)	0 month (0–1 month)
Babbles 'Da-da' and 'Ma-ma'	7 months (4–8 months)	4 months (2–6 months)
Responds to simple instructions	16 months (12–24 months)	10 months (6–14 months)
First word spoken with meaning	18 months (13–36 months)	14 months (10–23 months)
Two-word phrases	30 months (18–60+ months)	20 months (15–30 months)

Developmental milestones for children with Down syndrome

Milestone	Average age (and range) for children with Down syndrome	Average age (and range) for typically developing children
Social/self-help		
Smiles when talked to	2 months (1.5–4 months)	1 month (1–2 months)
Plays pat-a-cake or peek-a-boo	11 months (9–16 months)	8 months (5–13 months)
Drinks from ordinary cup unassisted	36 months (18–50+ months)	12 months (9–17 months)
Dry by day	36 months (18–50+ months)	24 months (14–36 months)
Bowel control	36 months (18–50+ months)	24 months (16–48 months)

Appendix C: Medical service providers

Here I provide details for the medical service providers you will potentially come in contact with once you receive your diagnosis for your child and as you help them be the best they can be.

Doctors and medical specialists

This section outlines the main types of doctors and medical specialists involved in the initial diagnosis and ongoing care for your child with disabilities or developmental delays.

General practitioners

General practitioners are doctors with generalist training who usually work in community-based medical practices (GP clinics). General practitioners are often involved in child development screening, immunisations and looking after children when they have general childhood illnesses such as viruses, colds, ear infections and coughs. If a child has a developmental delay or disability, a general practitioner might identify the developmental concern, but not commonly give a child a diagnosis of a specific disability. Instead, GPs will usually refer a child onto a paediatrician or other medical specialist for their further opinion and to decide on a diagnosis. If a child has a developmental delay and disability, the GP may be involved in the care of the child during simple acute illnesses, such as coughs and colds.

Paediatricians

Paediatricians are doctors who have done advanced training in a wide range of childhood illnesses, health conditions and disabilities.

Paediatricians can frequently give a child a diagnosis, but may refer the child onto other specialists if the diagnosis is not simple or clear. The paediatrician is then often the main medical doctor involved in the care of children with developmental delays and disabilities, although the paediatrician will often refer to and consult with other specialists for specialised care of different conditions associated with the diagnosis. For example, many children with cerebral palsy will have a general paediatrician who oversees the general care of the child's disability, who they see once to a few times a year to monitor and manage the child's general condition. But the child may also see a neurologist for their seizures, a rehabilitation physician for botox injections, and an orthopaedic surgeon if they require surgery at any point. A child with Down syndrome might see a paediatrician for their general ongoing monitoring and management, but might also see an optometrist or ophthalmologist for their eyesight and a cardiologist for their associated heart condition.

Neurologists

Neurologists are medical doctors who have done advanced training in assessment and management of the brain, spinal cord and nerves of the body. A neurologist may be involved in the diagnosis of neurological conditions, such as cerebral palsy, seizures, genetic peripheral neuropathies, cranial malformations, paediatric stroke, and other conditions affecting the brain, spinal cord and nerves. Neurologists are involved in the ongoing management of seizures, and will be involved in the care of children who have degenerative neurological conditions such as multiple sclerosis, peripheral neuropathies or myopathies.

Rehabilitation physicians or paediatricians

Rehabilitation physicians or paediatricians are doctors who have completed advanced training in the diagnosis and management of paediatric rehabilitation conditions, such as cerebral palsy, brain injury, neurodegenerative conditions, amputations (either congenital – that is, for children who are born with it – or traumatic). They also oversee rehabilitation following brain surgery, and rehabilitation following meningococcal septicaemia. The difference between a rehabilitation physician and a neurologist is the rehabilitation physician is more involved in the ongoing rehabilitation and development of children, whereas a neurologist is more involved in initial diagnosis of neurological conditions and then ongoing management of seizures. For example, a child may see a neurologist initially who may provide a diagnosis. The neurologist may then refer the child to the rehabilitation physician for the ongoing management of the condition. But the neurologist might continue to monitor and manage the child's seizures. Depending on the expertise and experience of your child's neurologist or rehab physician, their roles might also overlap.

Genetic specialists

Geneticists or genetic specialists are doctors who have done advanced training in the identification and diagnosis of genetic conditions. Your child may be referred to a geneticist if it is thought an underlying genetic condition is contributing to or causing their developmental delays or disabilities. Most doctors and paediatric therapists are usually able to identify some signs or features in a child that might indicate the possibility of an underlying genetic condition; it is the geneticist's job to look carefully for all the possible signs or features and put them together to form an idea of what the underlying condition might be, and then order the appropriate tests to try to identify the specific underlying condition.

Geneticists are also involved in genetic counselling for parents whose child has been diagnosed with a genetic condition who want to go on and have more children but might be at risk of having another child with the same condition. Geneticists are not usually involved with any reproductive or conception care, and are often not involved in the ongoing care of children with developmental delays and disabilities unless the child's condition cannot be identified initially – they might continue to follow up children who do not have a definitive diagnosis because, as research and scientific understanding of genetic conditions progress, the child's underlying genetic condition may be uncovered.

Neonatologists

Neonatologists are medical doctors who are specially trained in the management of newborn babies and babies born prematurely. Neonatologists usually work in the neonatal intensive care unit and special care nurseries, and care for babies during their admission to these units. Neonatologists are often not involved in the care of children following their discharge from these units, unless they are following up with children post-discharge for monitoring or research purposes.

Ophthalmologist

Ophthalmologists are medical doctors who have completed advanced training in the diagnosis, monitoring and management of eye conditions, including surgical management. Your child might be referred to an ophthalmologist if concern exists they are not seeing well, or if they have a condition such as strabismus (a condition where the eyes don't point in the same direction) that requires surgery. Ophthalmologists are often involved in diagnosing visual conditions in young children and children with developmental delays and disabilities involving brain damage that might cause a cortical visual impairment.

Therapists or allied health professionals

This section outlines the primary specialty areas of each of the different therapist involved in your child's care. However, many therapists who work in the field of paediatrics adopt a transdisciplinary approach. This means that each of your child's therapists might crossover and cover some of the care that your child's other therapists might focus on. For example, during a physiotherapy session you might find that as well as working on your child's movement skills, your child's physiotherapist might also work on your child's play, interaction, communication, problem-solving or fine motor skills. In addition, during your child's occupational therapy session, as well as working on dressing or handwriting skills, your child's occupational therapist might also do some activities to improve their core strength and practise their communication skills.

Optometrist

Optometrists are health professionals who are trained in assessing, diagnosing and managing conditions of the eye. We usually see an optometrist to determine if we need to wear glasses, but they can also diagnose conditions related to the eye health such as glaucoma or cataracts, and can also be involved in the diagnosis and care of children with learning conditions that might be due to their vision such as dyslexia. The differences between an optometrist and an ophthalmologist (covered in the 'Doctors and medical specialists' section) is that ophthalmologists are medical doctors who have completed advanced training in understanding the visual system, which includes the eye, the visual nerves, and the areas of the brain related to vision. Optometrists are not doctors, and their specialty is in the management of eye conditions such as visual clarity (how clearly your child can see), or eye health. If you child has a suspected cortical visual impairment (where they have a brain injury affecting the visual areas of their brain and how well their brain can interpret the images the eyes are seeing), you are more likely to see an ophthalmologist. If you child requires any kind of surgery on the eye or the structures associated with the eye, that will be performed by an ophthalmologist.

Physiotherapists

Physiotherapists are health professionals with training in the management of movement conditions. Physiotherapists who work in the field of paediatrics have knowledge and skills in understanding how children move, and providing therapy to help children to move better.

Occupational therapists

Occupational therapists are health professionals whose focus of assessment and intervention is on all the activities children might need to do in a certain day (a child's 'occupation' is all the things a child is required to do in their life). Occupational therapists often work on things like activities of daily living (such as dressing, toileting, bathing, eating and drinking, and preparing meals), behaviour, hand function (being able to use cutlery, write, reach, grasp and release), and play skills (which can include exploration of their environment and things in it, interacting and engaging with the people and the things in their environment, and imaginative play).

Speech pathologists

Speech pathologists are health professionals who are involved in assessing and managing your child's communication (which includes speech, language, comprehension and social skills), eating and drinking skills (in terms of how your child manages the food and drinks in their mouth and their swallowing).

Music therapists

Music therapists are health professionals who use music to engage children in therapy that helps them to develop and achieve their goals. For example, a music therapist might help a child to be able to learn to take turns when communicating with others, or they might help a child to practise their reaching and engaging with toys by using musical activities such as strumming a guitar or banging a drum or pressing a piano key. Music therapists can also work to improve a child's confidence and ability to participate in social interactions by engaging them in reciprocal interactions and participating in activities with others.

Social workers

Social workers are health professionals involved in supporting children with developmental disabilities and their families to be able to cope, thrive and meet their needs as a child and family. Social workers can be involved in helping to counsel families when their child is diagnosed with a condition, or when experiencing difficulties in their child's care or their family life. Social workers can also support families to get the help they need by providing information or linking them with community or specialty supports and services. Social workers are also often involved in advocating for a child's or family's needs if the parents require help with this.

Psychologists

Psychologists are health professionals involved in supporting children with how they think, feel, behave and learn. For example, a psychologist may support children experiencing anxiety, difficult behaviours such as anger, learning difficulties, self-esteem issues or difficulties in how they relate to their parents, siblings, peers or others. Psychologists can also support parents and other family members with their own thoughts and feelings, as well as their relationships with their children.

Other early intervention workers

As part of your child's ongoing care, you may also come into contact with the carers and teachers covered in this section.

Community health or community-based nurses

Community health or community-based nurses are involved in early childhood support and monitoring, early childhood and school-age immunisation programs, and can also be school-based nurses involved in supporting school-aged children within the school environment. Community health nursing services run screening programs where they conduct assessments to identify developmental difficulties and organise referrals to doctors and therapists for further assessment and intervention.

Early developmental education teachers

Early education teachers are university-trained teachers who have completed additional training in supporting children with developmental delays and disabilities in their early childhood learning. Early developmental education teachers might work within specific early childhood programs for children with diagnosed developmental delays or disabilities (an early childhood equivalent of a special school), or within mainstream services supporting children with developmental delays and disabilities. Early developmental education teachers are also involved in supporting families in deciding which school is best suited to their child with a developmental delay or disabilities.

Support workers

Some young children with more severe developmental delays and disabilities may also have support workers involved in their care. Support workers are workers who provide additional support in their child's usual environments, such as at home or at day care, kindy and school.

Appendix D: Funding options while accessing treatment

A number of funding options are available for your child to enable them to get early access to treatment. *Note:* The funding options I cover here are for residents of Australia.

Public health services

Public health services such as hospitals and community health programs do offer some health and developmental services for children with developmental delays and disabilities. Many children with conditions present from birth will start out receiving services from the public health system because the public health system often has neonatal units, special care nurseries, and baby follow-up clinics as part of their service. As the models for funding have changed in Australia (particularly as a result of the introduction of the NDIS), the types of services provided by the public health system have become more focused on managing the health-related concerns associated with a child's disability, such as feeding, spasticity, seizures and cardiorespiratory complications, with fewer supports available for significant rehabilitation beyond the early period of a child's (or adult's) condition. As a result, many children who start by being supported by the public health system are often transitioned out of the public health system for the bulk of their therapies, although the public health system will still be involved in managing their health-related issues.

Medicare Enhanced Primary Care (EPC)/Chronic Disease Management Plans (CDMP)

Medicare, Australia's national health care system, does provide some supports for children (and adults) with chronic health conditions. The term 'chronic health condition' is defined by Medicare as being a condition that has been present for at least six months or more, or is likely to be present for at least six months or more, and requires the services of more than one type of health professional (that is, requires both physio and podiatry, or requires both occupational therapy and speech therapy). If your child has a chronic health condition (and all developmental delays and disabilities should fall within that definition), your child can be eligible for up to five subsidised allied health therapy sessions per calendar year. In October 2019, the subsidy was $53.80. This means that Medicare will fund up to $53.80 for the session, and you need to pay the gap for any cost above $53.80 (unless the practice bulk bills, which means they only charge the $53.80 for the session). The EPC/CDMP is a good option for you to be able to get started with some therapy, or to complete some assessments if your child has not had access to the public health system for these. However, for children with developmental delays or disabilities, who more often than not will require ongoing care, the five sessions is usually only a good starting point.

Private health insurance

In Australia, individuals and families can pay for private health insurance that gives them coverage for hospital admission expenses, and can also provide subsidies or rebates for accessing outpatient type services such as specialist appointments and therapy appointments. Each individual fund will give different rebate amounts per session, depending on what coverage you have, and many will also have a capped amount of rebates you can claim per year (so if you spend over the capped amount, no rebate will be available). Check with your individual provider regarding what rebates are available for each of the health professionals your child needs to see, or shop around to see which health fund provides the best rebate for the lowest premium, and also covers the services your child needs. *Note:* At the time of writing, some health insurance rebates are lower than the Medicare rebate of $53.80 available through the EPC/CDMPs. Check with your health insurance provider what rebate is included in any cover you're considering; if it is lower than the Medicare rebate, getting an EPC/CDMP in the first instance might be worthwhile. For more information about rebates available, please contact each individual insurance company.

National Disability Insurance Scheme

The Australian National Disability Insurance Scheme (NDIS) is a relatively new funding scheme for eligible people with a disability who are residents of Australia. The scheme is designed to provide funding to people with a disability to enable them to maximise their functional and participation outcomes, so that they can increase their economic and social participation within our communities. To be eligible for funding through the scheme, you must have a permanent lifelong disability that affects your daily life. The scheme has quite a rigorous eligibility process that requires assessment or evidence of your child's level of disability and the supports they require to build their capacity and live their daily life. While the NDIS is still going through some teething problems (because it was only recently introduced), the scheme does offer some significant benefits in terms of children and adults being able to access supports and services that were not previously available, and promoting the choice and control of people with a disability to spend their funding the way they choose (as long as they are spending it on things that will enhance their capacity and help them live productive and meaningful lives). For more information please see: www.ndis.gov.au/.

Early childhood or school-aged education programs and supports

State governments in Australia are still responsible for providing supports and services to children with a disability within the education system. If your child has a diagnosed developmental delay or disability, they may be eligible to attend one of the state-funded programs available for early childhood education (before school age), or they might be eligible to access supports within their school environment that will help them to manage and get the most out of their time at school. To determine if your child might be eligible for these services, speak to your child's early childhood education provider, your child's school, or your child's therapist.

Other not-for-profit or non-government organisations providing government funded care

This type of government funding of large organisations or agencies to provide early intervention care is decreasing, likely in response to the shift in funding away from organisations and over to individuals with disability under the NDIS. However, checking if any agencies in your area are providing funded early childhood interventions can be worthwhile, especially if you are waiting for services through the public system or waiting on NDIS funding.

Charities

Some charities in Australia do raise funds to provide supports to children with developmental delays and disabilities. Similar to the not-for-profit or non-government organisations, check if any charities in your area or for children with developmental delay or disability in general might be able to provide funding for your child to access early childhood interventions, especially if you are waiting on supports through other systems such as the public system or the NDIS.

www.ingramcontent.com/pod-product-compliance
Lightning Source LLC
Chambersburg PA
CBHW071223080526
44587CB00013BA/1476